Better Trade for Sustainable Development:

The role of voluntary sustainability standards

Developing Countries in International Trade Studies

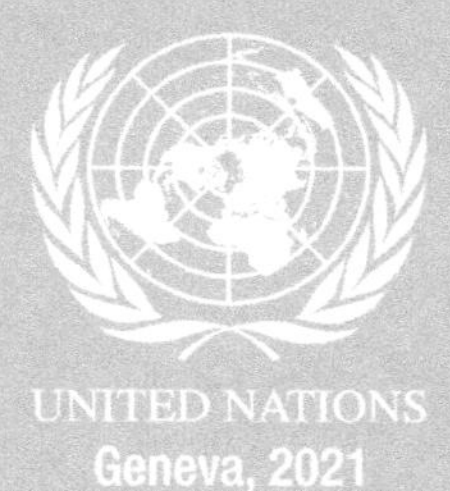

UNITED NATIONS
Geneva, 2021

United Nations publication issued by the United Nations Conference on Trade and Development.

UNCTAD/DITC/TAB/2021/2

ISBN: 978-92-1-113024-9
eISBN: 978-92-1-005886-5
Sales No.: E.21.II.D.20

CONTENTS

ACKNOWLEDGEMENTS

The study has been prepared by Axel Marx (Leuven Centre for Global Governance Studies, University of Leuven), Thomas Dietz (Institute of Political Science, University of Münster), Niematallah E. A. Elamin and Santiago Fernández de Cordoba from the Trade Analysis Branch (TAB) of the Division on International Trade and Commodities (DITC) at the United Nations Conference on Trade and Development (UNCTAD). The study benefited from comments and suggestions from Ralf Peters from the Trade Analysis Branch, DITC/UNCTAD. The study was formatted by Jenifer Tacardon-Mercado (UNCTAD).

EXECUTIVE SUMMARY

The 2030 Agenda for Sustainable Development of the United Nations constitutes the most important and comprehensive global sustainable development agenda for the next decade. It is known for its far-reaching and ambitious vision with its 17 sustainable development goals (SDGs) and 169 targets that are listed as part of the so-called "universal policy agenda" (United Nations, 2015). In the 2015 Agenda, and especially in SDG 17, international trade is singled out as a key policy instrument to contribute to all other SDGs. The 2030 Agenda for Sustainable Development defines international trade as "an engine for inclusive economic growth and poverty reduction, [that] contributes to the promotion of sustainable development". In order to become a 'sustainable engine' one approach that seems to be increasingly used is to internalize social, economic and environmental concerns in international trade. This can be done by many different means and policy instruments and tools. In this report we focus on a specific tool, namely Voluntary Sustainability Standards (VSS) which comprise of certification schemes, labeling programs and private standards. VSS aim to make global value chains, from producer to consumer, more sustainable by taking into account social and environmental requirements in the production process. VSS also often link developing countries (where many producers are based) to developed countries.

This report discusses in-depth the possibilities and limitations of VSS to make international trade more sustainable, in particular with regards to developing countries development opportunities. We first introduce the key concepts of trade, global value chains, sustainable development, their interrelatedness and their importance for developing countries. We focus on the rise of international trade and the changing nature of trade which is characterized by the dominance of global value chains. The emergence of global value chains allows producers in developing countries to be integrated in global economic dynamics which can contribute to their economic development. In addition, global value chains allow for the diffusion of social and environmental standards throughout production processes. VSS play an important role in this diffusion of social and environmental standards. We argue that global value chains can be governed in a way which enhances economic, social and environmental 'upgrading', i.e. a process by which negative social and environmental consequences are addressed in global value chains and which contributes to better protection of social and environmental standards. We show that upgrading through the governance of global value chains directly allows producers in developing countries to access global markets and reap their potential benefits contributing in this way to economic development in developing countries.

Then, the study zooms in on the role of VSS and shows that in order to consider VSS as tools for making value chains more sustainable it is important to understand that the concept of VSS captures a diversity of initiatives. And that not all VSS are equal in terms of design and effectiveness. We also discuss the drivers for VSS adoption in order to better understand their potential as tools for social and environmental upgrading of producers in developing countries. The report highlights that the use of VSS is driven by multiple drivers which influence the uptake of VSS. In addition, we also show, importantly from the perspective of developing countries, that this uptake is uneven and that there are several barriers to VSS uptake which specifically play out in the context of developing countries which do not always have the resources and capacity to comply with sustainability standards. These barriers relate to the costs involved in obtaining VSS, a lack of incentives, a governance gap and a distrust towards VSS. Some possible approaches to address these barriers are presented and discussed.

The report also focuses on the impact of VSS on the ground, mostly in developing countries. The more profound this impact is, the more VSS contribute to improved trading relations and facilitate sustainable development. From a policy perspective that aims to improve and foster more sustainable trade relations, especially between developing and developed countries, it thus presents a pivotal issue to assess the extent to which VSS indeed reach the goals that motivated their creation. In their theories of change, VSS define the causal steps (impact pathways) which, they theorize, lead from standard development to tangible changes towards more sustainable modes production at the ground level of certified production.

The study is concluded by policy recommendations. We argue that the potential of VSS to make trade more sustainable relies on two crucial components: first they need generate a substantial impact on the ground with regard to key sustainability parameters (impact-dimension). Second, in order to enhance their impact they need to be widely used (adoption-dimension). In order to improve on both dimensions, we discuss in the recommendations four more structural approaches/transformations which can be considered for enhancing the potential of VSS. First, we introduce the supporting role of donors and multilateral organizations. Second, we focus on the further integration of VSS in public policies. Third, we discuss actions to further harness the market-based potential of VSS by providing more transparency to consumers. And fourth, we consider strengthening the empowerment potential of VSS to create stronger incentives for producers and other actors to use and adopt VSS.

1. INTRODUCTION

The 2030 Agenda for Sustainable Development of the United Nations constitutes the most important and comprehensive global sustainable development agenda for the next decade. It is known for its far-reaching and ambitious vision with its 17 sustainable development goals (SDGs) and 169 targets that are listed as part of the so-called "universal policy agenda" (United Nations, 2015). The Agenda marks a new approach in the United Nations governance model as it further develops and embraces 'governance through goals' (Biermann et al. 2017), building on the approach taken in the Millennium Development Goals (MDGs). The SDGs need to be achieved by different policy approaches and instruments. In the 2015 Agenda, and especially in SDG 17, international trade is singled out as a key policy instrument to contribute to all other SDGs. The 2030 Agenda for Sustainable Development defines international trade as "an engine for inclusive economic growth and poverty reduction, [that] contributes to the promotion of sustainable development".

The expansion of international trade in the last decades although has brought economic and societal benefits across the globe, it led sometimes to fail in addressing the adverse social and environmental and even economic impacts. In order for trade to become a 'sustainable engine' one approach that seems to be increasingly used is to *internalize* social, economic and environmental concerns in international trade. This can be done by many different means and policy instruments and tools. In this report we focus on a specific tool, namely Voluntary Sustainability Standards (VSS) which comprise of certification schemes, labeling programs and private standards (Marx et al., 2012). VSS have become, over the last three decades, an important transnational governance instrument (Abbott and Snidal, 2009) and aim to make global value chains, from producer to consumer, more sustainable by taking into account social and environmental requirements in the production process. VSS also often link developing countries (where many producers are based) to developed countries.

This report provides a comprehensive analysis of the potentials and constraints of VSS in making international trade more sustainable, in particular with regards to developing countries development opportunities. In the second chapter we first highlight a twofold evolution in international trade over the last 5 decades. On the one hand we show that international trade increased significantly over the last five decades. Although shocks like the oil crisis in the 1970s, the financial crisis in 2008 and the pandemic have had a negative impact on the growth of trade, overall we observe a significant growth in international trade from 1970s onwards. The exponential increase in global trade has enabled many, though by far not all, developing countries to pursue economic development through export and export diversification. On the other hand, we observe that the nature of trade has changed and that products are now made by bringing parts together from different parts of the world. The emergence of global value chains allows producers in developing countries to be integrated in global economic dynamics which can contribute to their economic development. In addition, global value chains allow for the diffusion of social and environmental standards throughout production processes. VSS, as we will argue, play an important role in this diffusion of social and environmental standards.

Next, we delve into the relationship between trade and sustainable development and highlight the possible positive and negative economic, social and environmental consequences of trade. We argue that global value chains can be governed in a way which enhances economic, social and environmental 'upgrading', *i.e.* a process by which negative social and environmental consequences are addressed in global value chains and which contributes to better protection of social and environmental standards. Upgrading through the governance of global value chains directly allows producers in developing countries to access global markets and reap their potential benefits contributing in this way to economic development in developing countries.

An increasingly important instrument to govern global value chains are VSS which is the focus of chapter 3. The chapter introduces how VSS work, explores their diversity and analyses the drivers for VSS adoption. In addition, it highlights that the use of VSS is driven by multiple drivers which influence the uptake of VSS.

It also shows that this uptake is uneven and that there are several barriers to VSS uptake which specifically play out in the context of developing countries. Some of the actions which can be taken to overcome these barriers are also highlighted and presented.

Chapter 4 turns to the impact of VSS on the ground, mostly in developing countries. It starts out by providing a stylized version of the theory of change which underpins the work of VSS and provides a structured overview of the literature to date that has evaluated the impacts of VSS on sustainable trade and production. The final part of chapter 4 explains some of the major challenges that VSS face in becoming more effective.

The final chapter focuses on policy recommendations with a focus on the role of donors and multilateral organizations, integrating VSS in public policies, enhancing transparency of VSS to consumers, and strengthening the empowerment potential of VSS.

2. TRADE, GLOBAL VALUE CHAINS AND SUSTAINABLE DEVELOPMENT

2.1 TRADE AND GVCS: CONNECTING DEVELOPING COUNTRIES PRODUCERS WITH GLOBAL MARKETS

The importance of global value chains (GVCs) for international trade is commonly recognized. Indeed, the nature of international trade changed in the last decades. *"Steadily declining costs of trade and information and telecommunications have permitted firms to geographically splinter their 'production lines', designing international supply chains that allocate different parts of the production process to firms in different countries. (Hoekman, 2014, p. 15)"*. It is through global value chains that VSS are able to diffuse social and environmental standards globally. In this section, we first delve into the importance and relevance of GVCs for international trade.

Powered by the rise of global supply or value chains international trade expanded rapidly after 1990, (see Figure 1). Today, around 70 per cent of international trade involves global value chains, where parts and components are exchanged across countries before being incorporated into final products (OECD, 2020). GVCs can make it easier for countries, to diversify away from primary products to manufactures and services, and can also enhance their ability to exploit their comparative advantage. GVCs trade exhibits two features that distinguish it from traditional trade: hyper specialization and durable firm-to-firm relationships. These features allow firms to raise productivity and income, rendering GVC trade more powerful than traditional trade in supporting growth and poverty reduction (World Bank, 2020).

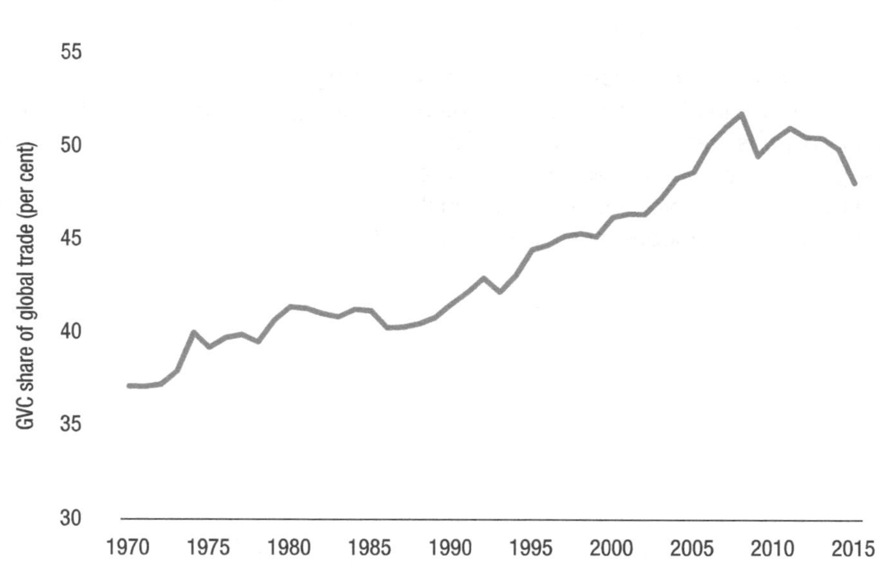

Figure 1. GVC share of global trade 1970 – 2015

Source: World development report (2020).

When it comes to measurement of GVC participation, the traditional approach is to look at bilateral trade in intermediate products. Trade in intermediates is a key characteristic of value chain activity and has considerable data availability and detail advantages (Kowalski et al., 2015).[1] UNCTAD (2019a) mentions that intermediate products represent almost half of the world goods trade (see Figure 2) and continued to make up the bulk of world trade in 2018 (about US$ 8.3 trillion in 2018), with consumer products amounting to about a quarter (US$ 4.8 trillion in 2018).

---

[1] A shortcoming is that it does not trace the origin and use of intermediates which can come from third countries and can be used by them for either further export processing or consumption. For more see Participation-Developing-Countries-GVCs-Summary-Paper-April-2015.pdf (oecd.org)

Figure 2. Exports and imports value by stage of processing (2018)

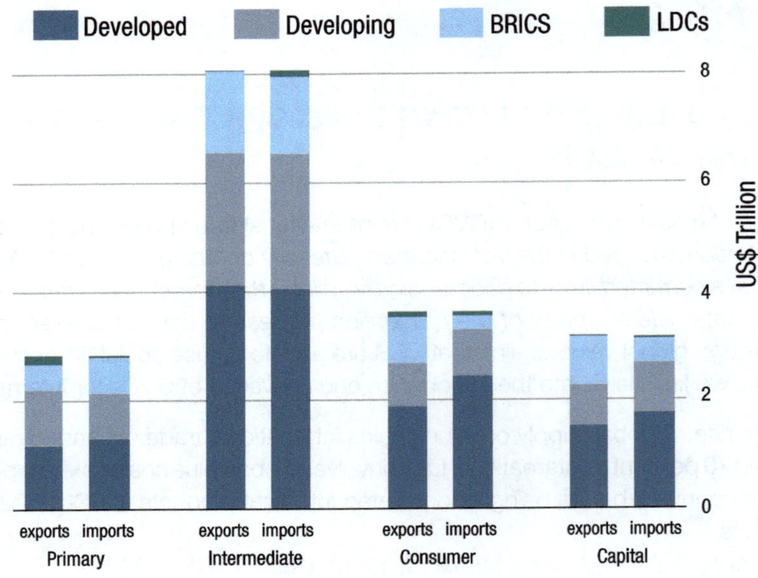

Source: UNCTAD, Key Statistics and Trends in International Trade 2019.

Figure 3 demonstrates the level of developing countries trade in intermediate goods (as a percentage of world's trade). In 2019, developing countries, excluding china, accounted for 26 per cent and 30 per cent of the global exports and imports of intermediate goods, respectively. China alone, accounts for around 11 per cent of the global exports as well as imports of intermediate goods. LDCs share in global exports stood at 1 per cent in the last decade. Moreover, LDCs participation in global value chains has often been limited to the lowest rungs of the chain, with modest ensuing benefits (UNCTAD, 2018).

Figure 3. Share of developing countries intermediate goods exports and imports (1996-2019)

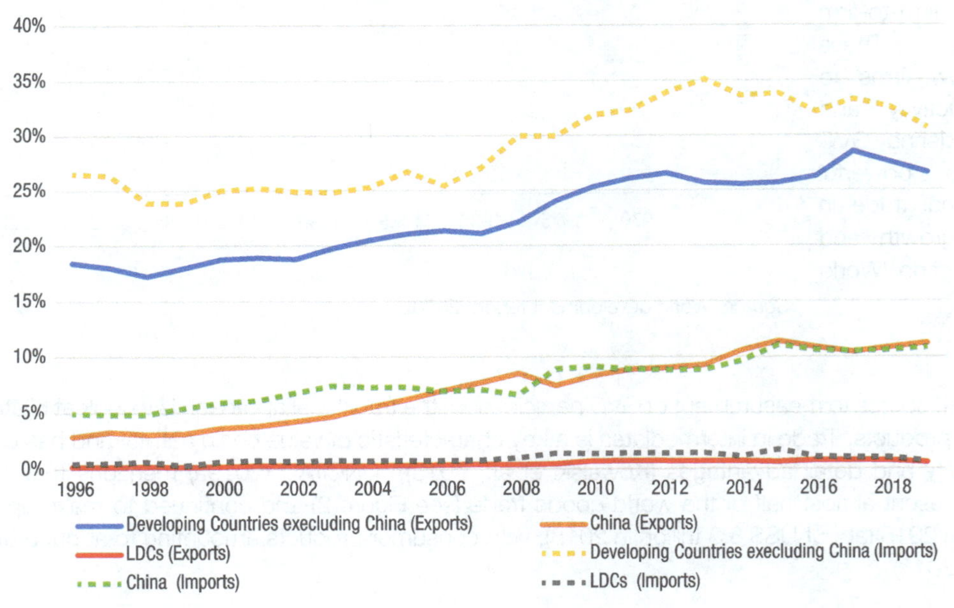

Source: Authors' calculation based on data from UNcomtrade.

Kowalski et al. (2015) looked at the participation of developing countries into GVCs, finds that structural characteristics of countries are the main determinants of GVC participation. Policy also can nevertheless play a significant role. The latest World Development Report (2020) indicates that GVC participation is determined by fundamentals such as factor endowments, market size, geography, and institutional quality.

Nevertheless, there is an ongoing debate about the extent and desirability of integration into regional and global value chains and the benefits associated with wider participation for developing countries (e.g., UNCTAD, 2014). For instance, WTO (2019) looked at implications of GVCs integration for workers in developing countries, in terms of jobs and wages, sector of employment, and skills. It is found that the employment creation and wage gains through a higher GVCs participation have been biased towards more skilled workers in developing countries, which contrasts with the predictions of trade theory. In addition, UNCTAD (2019b) identified several factors showing how trade has contributed to reduce between country and increase within country inequalities.

Furthermore, when considering the economic losses from environmental damages and social distortions that may have been caused by GVCs, it could be said that integration into GVCs doesn't inevitably result in overall economic upgrade. The coming section discusses the issue of trade and sustainable development in the era of global value chains.

2.2 TRADE AND SUSTAINABLE DEVELOPMENT: RACE TO THE BOTTOM VERSUS RACE TO THE TOP

International trade can bring prosperity but potentially also create negative social and environmental consequences through direct effects (scale effects) and indirect effects (increased competition which generates pressures to cut production costs) (Irwin, 2020; WTO, 2018). The economic and social benefits of trade have been detailed by many economists and are multifold. They include export-led economic growth, economic diversification and restructuring (vertical integration), industrialization, efficient resource allocation, positive income effects, technological innovation and poverty alleviation. Other authors have also identified non-economic benefits of trade on peace and democratic institutions. Going back to the work of Montesquieu and John Stuart Mill some authors have developed the capitalist peace theory, which states that trade makes countries more commercially interdependent and provides strong incentives to avoid war. Also, the relationship between trade, economic development and democracy has received significant scholarly attention.

The effects of trade on social and environmental protection have long been recognized in policy reports and academic literature. For example, the International Labour Organization was established in 1919 to produce international norms on a range of labour-related issues to prevent a global race to the bottom of labour rights in a world which saw increasing international competition and trade (Mahaim, 1934; Servais, 2011). It was feared that increased trade and investment could lead to a deterioration of labour rights such as working hours, safety of workers, wages, etc. The fear has been that the positive consequences of trade (more economic growth) would be off-set by negative social consequences. The fear of using (lowering or not enforcing) social standards to achieve competitive advantage was also discussed by the World Commission on the Social Dimension of Globalization which stated that *"no country should achieve or maintain comparative advantage based on ignorance of, or deliberate violations of, core labour standards"* (World Commission on the Social Dimension of Globalization, 2004, para. 421). Similarly, concerns were voiced on the impact of international trade on environmental pollution and the protection of natural resources. For example, according to the Global Environment Facility (GEF), three widely traded commodities (soy, beef and palm oil) are responsible for close to 80 per cent of tropical deforestation worldwide and for 12 per cent of greenhouse gas emissions globally. (GEF, 2014)

This nexus between trade and sustainable development concerns has led several authors to consider that increased international trade might lead to a race to the bottom with regard to social (Mosley, 2011; Cuyvers & De Meyer, 2012) and environmental protection (Potoski and Prakash, 2005). Although there is some evidence on negative effects of increased trade on the protection of labour rights and the environment, several authors have also argued that the increase in trade might lead to a race to the top for better social and environmental

protection (Vogel, 2005; Garcia-Johnson, 2000). The mechanisms by which trade might lead to a spread of stricter environmental and social standards was recently elaborated by Bradford (2020). She highlights the importance of multi-national corporations and global value chains) to spread stricter social and environmental standards across the globe. Firms do this to streamline management and production practices and procedures and, in this way, reduce transaction costs. Rather than looking for locations with low social and environmental standards, firms are assumed to apply the social and environmental standards from the strictest jurisdiction and diffuse these other locations where they operate and even require suppliers to adhere to them. Hence, the mechanism via which social and environmental standards diffuse are global value chains.

GVCs have become a dominant feature of global trade, comprising developed, developing, emerging, and least developed economies. Decisions related to location of the facilities and sources of production inputs are determined based on the availability and obtainability of the essential skills and materials at a competitive cost and quality.

Box 1. Trade and Sustainable Development Goals

The Sustainable Development Goals (SDGs) are a holistic framework that define the international policy agenda. They cover a broad range of socio-economic, developmental, and environmental topics.

The 2030 Agenda for Sustainable Development defines international trade as "an engine for inclusive economic growth and poverty reduction, [that] contributes to the promotion of sustainable development". International trade is concerned with the efficient allocation of goods and capital, contributing to sustainability via productivity improvement and increased welfare (Dupuy and Agarwala, 2014). In addition, trade is regulated and influenced by a wide array of policies and instruments that act as policy interfaces between the SDGs and trade. These instruments include many forms of non-tariff measures (NTMs), as well as technical barriers to trade (TBT) and sanitary and phytosanitary measures (SPS). Over the last decades, Voluntary Sustainability Standards (VSS) have emerged as new market-based tools to address key sustainability challenges.

International trade, supported by strong international cooperation, embodied in the multilateral trading system, can be a powerful force for creating jobs (SDG 8; Decent Work and Economic Growth) fostering efficient use of resources, stimulating entrepreneurship and ultimately lifting people out of poverty (SDG 1; No Poverty). This results in industrialization and development, helping to achieve SDG 9 (Industry, Innovation and Infrastructure). Also, WTO rules try to reduce the impact of existing inequalities through the principle of Special and Differential Treatment for Developing Countries, which helps in attaining SDG 10 (Reduced Inequalities).

In addition, trade plays a critical role in addressing hunger, food security, nutrition and sustainable agriculture (SDG 2; Zero Hunger), contributing to healthy lives and wellbeing (SDG 3; Good Health and Well-Being), among others. Although social issues are currently not addressed at the multilateral level in the WTO, bilateral agreements, however, often address such issues. As many include labour clauses that promote the respect of workers' rights or gender equality (UNCTAD, 2019b) (SDGs 5; Gender Equality, and 10; Reduced Inequality).

Many trade policies and various WTO Agreements primarily aim at protecting health or the environment. About 10 per cent of all measures notified under the WTO SPS Agreement and the TBT Agreement cite environmental protection as one of their objectives, including controls on hazardous substances, air pollution or waste management. ESCAP and UNCTAD (2019) find that globally on average 41 per cent of NTMs directly and positively address SDGs.

... /...

However, benefiting from trade also presents challenges for developing and least developed countries (LDCs). The LDCs, despite their gradual integration into the world market, their share in world trade still stands at about 1 per cent. Inclusive trade requires an improvement in connectivity – both physical infrastructure and digital networks. Policymakers need to take proactive actions to channel trade and investment into activities and sectors that can help mitigate the environmental and social impacts while capturing the economic benefits.

A WTO report (2018) that focused on mainstreaming trade to achieve the SDGs provided recommendations on ways to accelerate progress in achieving the SDGs that include: mainstreaming trade into national and sector strategies to achieve the SDGs; strengthening the multilateral trading system so that it can continue supporting inclusive growth, jobs and poverty reduction; continue reducing trade costs including through full implementation of the WTO's Trade Facilitation Agreement; building supply-side capacity and trade-related infrastructure in developing countries and LDCs; focusing on export diversification and value addition; enhancing the services sector; applying flexible rules of origin to increase utilization of preference schemes; ensuring that non-tariff measures do not become barriers to trade; making e-commerce a force for inclusion; and supporting micro, small and medium-sized enterprises to engage in international trade.

2.3 ECONOMIC, SOCIAL AND ENVIRONMENTAL UPGRADING THROUGH GLOBAL VALUE CHAINS

As noted GVCs play an important role in international trade and are the mechanism by which VSS diffuse standards. These GVCs take different forms (Gereffi et al., 2005; Gereffi & Fernandez-Stark, 2011; Ponte, 2019). Each has distinct governance arrangements and power relations which affect the degree to which sustainability concerns, *i.e.* economic, environmental, and social issues, can be addressed in the value chain. Depending on the governance of GVCs social and environmental standards can be up- or downgraded throughout the value chain. Several observers see opportunities to foster sustainable development and responsible business practices by enabling lead firms in GVCs to engage in social and environmental upgrading. Social upgrading refers to '*improvements in labour-related standards, such as wages, working hours, worker's safety and others which contribute to better social conditions and quality of life for workers*' (Ponte, 2019, p. 138). Environmental upgrading refers to '*a process of improving or minimizing the environmental impact of GVC operations, including production, processing, distribution, consumption and disposal, reuse and recycling*' (Ponte, 2019, p. 142).

Social and environmental upgrading can occur to varying degrees, be initiated by different drivers and occur through different pathways. Concerning degrees upgrading can be pursued in a superficial or shallow way or in an embedded way. The former refers to practices in which lead firms only require minimal adjustments to existing social and environmental standards. The latter refers to types of engagement between lead firms and other firms in the global value chain which really aim to make a transformation towards sustainable development possible. Concerning drivers for social and environmental upgrading. Ponte (2019) and Gereffi and Lee (2014) identify 5 drivers namely consumer demand, business to business demand for reputation management, civil society (unions and environmental groups) pressure, public regulation and multi-stakeholder collaboration to address sustainability issues. Finally concerning pathways. Social and environmental upgrading can occur through the integration of social and environmental considerations in the production process or through vertical integration, i.e. a shift from, for example, smallholder contract-farming towards integrated estate farming which implements sustainability practices (Maertens and Swinnen, 2012; Loconto & Dankers, 2014).

Whether social and environmental upgrading throughout value chains will occur depends on the governance arrangement in the value chain and the position of the most powerful firms in the value chain. In buyer-driven commodity value chains which are dominated by Western brands or large retailers, the likelihood of upgrading increases. Large retailers or strong brands can often determine sustainability requirements downstream in the value chain. If these upstream actors require stronger sustainability commitments, this will play

out downstream in the value chain all the way to the producers. Given the relative importance Western retailers pay to sustainability concerns and the so-called 'supermarket revolution' whereby most products are sold through supermarkets giving them increased power in value chains (World Bank, 2008), this might influence the adoption of sustainability standards. However, there is also some evidence that intermediaries in the value chain are becoming more powerful and change the balance of power in value chains in two ways. First, as Levi et al (2012) note, some suppliers in some developing countries have specialized skills and know-how and have developed market niches in which they are dominant. It is not easy for 'Western' retailers to switch to other suppliers. In this context they need to negotiate the terms of cooperation, including taking sustainability concerns onboard, instead of stipulating them. Second, some of these firms have grown so fast, multiplying their customers (often large brands), that they no longer depend on one brand or retailer. Both dynamics increase the bargaining power of these firms in the value chain putting sometimes downward pressures on sustainability concerns. In addition, short-term ownership and mobility of factories in value chains might also affect sustainability considerations in value chains. In several manufacturing industries, factories, or capital sustaining them, are highly mobile and are searching constantly for locations with the lowest input costs, i.e. low social and environmental standards (Levi et al. 2012; O'Rourke, 2001). Hence, as Levi et al. (2012, p. 22) note: *"When challenged by workers forming unions or pressured by MNCs trying to induce compliance with private regulatory schemes, many factories will simply shut their doors without paying severance to workers and re-locate."* However, it should be noted that this relocation dynamic is not always supported by evidence and there are several counter examples. For example, Robertson et al. (2011), who analyzed factories in Cambodia which implemented more stringent labour standards, did not found that this influenced the probability of plant closure. They argued it might even increase the probability of plant survival which could be an effect of opening up markets demanding products made under more stringent labour standards.

Finally, a key challenge to social and environmental upgrading concerns the reach of sustainability requirements in the value chain or the degree a value chain can be penetrated. Sometimes producers in developing countries are second/third tiers suppliers which makes it difficult to reach them. Many large multinational firms do not only have thousands of suppliers but even these suppliers outsource, sometimes to thousands of homeworkers. The stitching of footballs provides an example. Although the football industry (manufacturers of footballs) is a quite consolidated sector with relatively few producers (and countries) involved (Nadvi, 2011), the effective making of a football involves many people. Thomsen and Nadvi (2010) analyzed two regions, Sialkot in Pakistan and Jalandhar in India, which provide footballs for different buyers including megabrands such as Adidas and Nike, but also other major retailers. In these two regions more than 500 businesses are active, which have in total 3400 subcontractors themselves, which in turn outsource the effective stitching of footballs to a few thousand stitchers. Hence, only the making of one product already requires reaching many thousands of entities. To do this in a systematic way is a very demanding task and the current structure of value chains might inhibit the realization of social and environmental objectives (Locke, 2013).

Box 2. COVID-19 and Global Value Chains

The COVID-19 crisis has led to a collapse in world trade and disruption to many GVCs. The nationwide lockdowns due to the spread of COVID-19 has forced developed and developing countries to halt their economies (Lambert et al., 2020). Moreover, COVID-19 has amplified profound fault lines in the functioning of global value chains (GVCs) and exposed the fragility of a model characterized by high interdependencies between leading firms and suppliers located across several continents (Fortunato, 2020).

A study by WTO (2021) conducted analysis of the reasons for changes in GVCs as a result of COVID-19 both from a positive angle and normative angle. It drew three main conclusions. First, the COVID-19 pandemic could contribute to diversification of sources of supply whose extent will vary by sector depending on the costs of value chain reorganization. Second, the pandemic has led to increased attention to the provision of essential goods in situations of crisis and the analysis concludes that to achieve this objective, global cooperation should be preferred to national policies such as domestic production and export restrictions. Third, the largest risk for the global economy in the aftermath of the pandemic is a move away from open, non-discriminatory trade policies, which would jeopardize the large benefits of open trade regimes in the current global economy characterized by scale economies, innovation spillovers, and a global division of labour (WTO, 2021).

Most analysts concur that the current pandemic will reinforce relocation and reshoring trends. Both might allow for more flexible adjustment to changing demand, and mitigating firms' risks in the event of external shocks (Fortunato, 2020)

A study by Castaneda-Navarrete et. al (2020) analyzed and characterized disruptions to the global apparel value chain caused by the COVID-19 pandemic and found that developing countries are suffering disproportionately in terms of profits, wages, job security, and job safety. Women worker in the apparel chain have been hit especially hard, not only because most workers in the chain are women, but also because they have experienced increasing unpaid care work and higher risk of gender-based violence.

In such a complicated and rapidly changing environment, developing countries need to concentrate their efforts around more diversification, strengthening regional value chains, and more state regulations (Fortunato, 2020).

3. SUSTAINABLE VALUE CHAINS: ROLE, TOOLS AND CHALLENGES

3.1 VOLUNTARY SUSTAINABILITY STANDARDS

The United Nations Forum on Sustainability Standards (UNFSS) (2013, p. 3) defines VSS as *"standards specifying requirements that producers, traders, manufacturers, retailers or service providers may be asked to meet, relating to a wide range of sustainability metrics, including respect for basic human rights, worker health and safety, the environmental impacts of production, community relations, land use planning and others."* VSS are considered as a significant transnational governance instruments to pursue sustainable development. Over the last decades the number of VSS has proliferated (UNFSS, 2020).

VSS can affect trade in different ways (Elamin and Fernandez de Cordoba, 2020). UNFSS (2018) shows that VSS affect trade through their effect on the structure of the market, and global value chain participation and structure. According to the literature, VSS can be catalysts or barriers to trade. On the one hand, VSS can lead to increased exports, as VSS provide a competitive advantage to complying producers and signal sustainable production practices that facilitate their market access to foreign markets. Masood & Brümmer (2014) link a favourable trade impact of VSS to the demand enhancing effect that takes place due to the safety and quality of certified products, product differentiation, and harmonization. In addition, VSS can be trade-enhancing as they reduce information asymmetries and transaction costs (Henson & Jaffee, 2008; Jaffee, 2003; Andersson, 2019), and modernize the value chains through innovation and upgrading (Swinnen, 2007). Next, VSS can bring benefits in the form of higher productivity and lower input costs (Graffham et al., 2007). On the other hand, some suggest that the expansion and increased influence of VSS have become an increasing concern for suppliers, in particular those in low-income countries. If VSS are de facto mandatory for specific markets, small-scale producers mainly risk being excluded from export value chains due to high compliance costs and increasing monitoring costs (Unnevehr, 2000; UNCTAD, 2008; Hobbs, 2010; Masood and Brümmer, 2014). We return to the issue of exclusion due a high cost later in the report when we discuss barriers for VSS uptake. Standards also affect the international competitiveness of domestic farmers, particularly in developing countries. If producers in developing countries are competing directly with producers in developed countries, and are in general less able to implement the requirements of VSS at a given level of cost, they could lose out (UNFSS, 2013). In sum, the main argument for voluntary standards having a negative impact on international trade revolves around the burden of compliance costs. On the other hand, as we note above, VSS are argued to help in reducing transaction costs between buyers and sellers and make trade more likely. Mangelsdorf (2011) and Swan (2010) argue that VSS reduce trade when the compliance costs outweigh transaction costs and foster trade vice versa.

How do VSS work?

VSS aim to ensure that products and production processes comply with a set of social and environmental requirements based on three distinct steps. First, VSS integrate elements of existing international rules and agreements into their own rules, standards and procedures. Many VSS start with developing a general mission and set of principles on which they are based. These principles often refer to international agreements and conventions. These conventions and agreements are the starting point for developing more precise standards. Second, VSS translate international norms and principles in specific standards and benchmarks, which makes compliance assessment possible. Often, VSS initiatives start by defining general principles and delegate the formulation of specific standards to working groups or committees which can take local conditions into account. This operationalization of international conventions into measurable standards is often very precise and allows the assessment of compliance with these standards. Third, VSS put systems in place to assess conformity with standards and monitor continuous compliance with standards. Conformity assessment is often performed by accredited third bodies (certification bodies). The initial conformity assessment of VSS is achieved via a system based on the development of management plans outlining how conformity with standards will be achieved by the applicant of a certificate and the control on the implementation of these plans by independent certifiers. This is done in five steps:

- Step one, the applicant invites an inspector who conducts a pre-audit or feasibility study on whether the entity under consideration can be certified.

- Step two, a genuine audit is conducted, which assesses the current management practices against the standards and criteria. This audit also can contain detailed corrective actions requests (CARs), which are necessary in order to gain certification.

- Step three involves implementing the corrective actions and an assessment of the audit by the applicant.

- Step four is a new audit, which often contains more corrective actions to be implemented.

- Step five finalises the process by awarding the certificate. First certificates can have a duration for only one year which then subsequently can be renewed for multiple years.

After the certification, conformity with standards is assessed via monitoring often based on auditing (by certification bodies) and complaint systems. Monitoring and auditing is outsourced to professional accredited organisations and companies. These monitors work with standardised procedures, which include an analysis of documents and site visits on the basis of surveys and checklists.

The above discussion illustrates that in the certification process several distinct actors play a role. Figure 4 summarizes how certification through VSS works. VSS, as standard-setters, develop standards which form the basis for a VSS certificate. Certificates are being issued upon a compliance assessment carried out by independent third-party auditors. Such auditors form part of a *certification body*. The work done by certification bodies is checked in an *accreditation* process and by an accreditation office which is appointed by a VSS. The accreditation office verifies whether the certification bodies are competent to perform the conformity assessment. The certification body awards the certificate to the standard-taker (producers, owner of natural resources) if the latter complies with all the standards.

Figure 4. **Stylized Presentation of Actors involved in Certification**

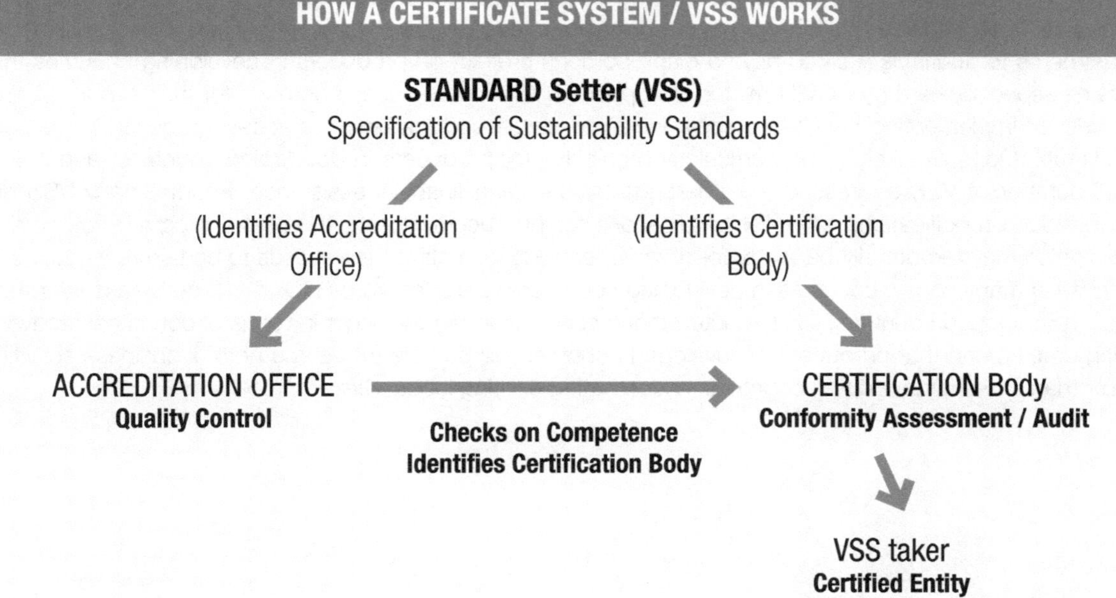

Box 3. COVID-19 and VSS

The impacts of COVID-19 have been felt across all sectors of business and at every stage of production, as supply chains have been disrupted and markets for final products and services have changed. Many private regulators engaged in sustainability governance, such as voluntary sustainability standards (VSS), have had to respond to these dynamics through adjustments to their own operations and business practices as well as to various commitments that they expect the operators they certify to meet. Because many of these operators are located in developing countries, pre-existing challenges common to producers in developing and emerging economies are likely to be intensified by the impacts of COVID-19. Research by Auld and Renckens (2021) into the responses to the COVID-19 pandemic of 84 VSS programs active in developing countries shows private regulators have taken a variety of approaches as they attempt to balance flexibility for their members in light of the health crisis with maintaining credibility and trust in their standard. Changes to policies for audits – the primary mechanism used by VSS to ensure compliance with their standards – were put into place by more than half of the VSS in the study, and most commonly included audit postponement / deadline extensions, a switch to conducting audits remotely, or both (Auld and Renckens, 2021, p. 5). Much less commonly, some VSS offered substantive adjustments to audits, including flexibility on reporting requirements or, in a few cases, temporarily easing certain rules or providing for COVID-related exemptions to compliance with certain indicators (ibid., pp. 5-6). While some adjustments were applied across the board, in several cases private regulators outlined specific limiting conditions for policy adjustments intended to take into account certain risks, such as an operator's prior instances of non-conformance or even country-level risks.

Auld and Renckens highlight that the changes introduced by private regulators in response to the outbreak of COVID-19 are likely to exacerbate existing inequalities between operators in developing and developed countries. First, the conditions that were placed on which operators could avail of temporary adjustments to audit policy (e.g. deadline extensions or submission of incomplete data) based on risk assessments are likely to disproportionately limit their use by operators in developing countries. This is especially true when country-level risk assessments are used; for example, a risk-assessment tool used by the Aquaculture Stewardship Council limited the use of remote audits for operators in countries deemed to be high risk – all of which were in the developing countries (Auld and Renckens 2021, p. 6). Second, most regulators' lack of flexibility with regard to performance rules (only seven in the study introduced substantive adjustments to audits) is likely to have a disproportionate effect on producers in developing countries that were hit especially hard by COVID-related disruptions, including decreased demand for their exports. Third, the cost of implementing new technology (including stable and fast internet access) required for remote and virtual audits are likely to be particularly prohibitive for producers in developing countries, and only a small number of VSS addressed this challenge by providing financial assistance. Fourth, many VSS did not introduce modifications for initial certifications for producers looking to enter a program for the first time, which may temporarily bar entry for these operators, restricting their access to certain markets. Fifth, because in many cases, countries in developing countries were affected by COVID-19 outbreaks later than those in developed countries, it is expected that a similar time-lag will occur in terms of countries' recovery, which could mean that producers in developed countries will be able to resume normal business activities earlier than those in developing countries, exacerbating existing inequalities.

3.2 VSS AS TOOLS FOR SUSTAINABLE VALUE CHAINS: UNDERSTANDING VSS DIVERSITY

When considering VSS as tools for sustainable value chains it is important to understand that the concept of VSS captures a diversity of initiatives. Several studies have been published on understanding this diversity and the "institutional" design of VSS, looking at the standard-setting process as well as the enforcement of standards. The way VSS are designed will to a degree influence their impact and uptake in developing countries. We return to this in section 3.3 and 4 of this paper. Four streams of research highlight different aspects of VSS which are relevant in the discussion on the role of VSS as a tool to make global value chains more sustainable.

A first stream focuses on the substance of standards and analyses on what social, economic and environmental aspects standards are set, and how stringent these standards are. (Holvoet and Muys, 2004). This line of research also focuses on which international norms, conventions and agreements these standards are based on. Concerning the latter, some authors argue that VSS are rooted in existing international law and in this way do not create any new rules or commitments but operationalise existing commitments to economic operators (Marx, 2017).

A second stream looks into who is involved in the standard-setting process. Some authors argue that VSS are remarkably democratic and inclusive in standard-setting (Dingwerth, 2007), while others are more sceptical and critical; and highlight that key-actors in the standard-setting process like producers are hardly represented in the standard-setting process (Bennett, 2017). The importance of inclusiveness in the standard-setting process is recognized by several VSS. Some initiatives have developed procedures to guarantee that the standard-setting process is inclusive following the guidelines developed by the ISEAL Alliance, which is a membership organization of some VSS which adhere to a set of principles, codes and standards of the ISEAL Alliance. The ISEAL Alliance proposes that *"The standard-setting organisation shall carry out a stakeholder mapping exercise [...] at the beginning of a standard development or revision process to identify major interest sectors and key interested parties, based on the standard's objectives"* (ISEAL Alliance, 2010, p. 7). In addition, the ISEAL recommends that *'key stakeholders shall be proactively approached to contribute to the consultations"* (ISEAL, 2010, p. 7)

A third stream of research focuses on how standards are enforced and conformity with standards is assessed focusing on the use of audit systems and complaint systems (Marx & Wouters, 2017). Concerning audits, studies focused on different aspects including the quality of information in auditing (Maquila Solidarity Network, 2005), the consequences of routinization which results in auditors doing a 'quick' job and missing crucial information (O'Rourke, 2000; Sabel et. al., 2000; Esbenshade, 2004),the sporadic nature of audits and the risk underreporting due to an inherent conflict of interests (auditors are paid by the business enterprises) (Lokce, 2013; Kim, 2012). Several authors argue that due to the dynamics in value chains, due to consumer demand, it is near impossible to assess conformity through annual audits. Locke (2013) provides several case studies of how global value chains work and the flexibility they require to remain competitive. This flexibility implies that workplace practices change very quickly which impact sustainability standards.

The deficiencies of the audit system led to the development of additional forms of monitoring and conformity assessment with a specific focus on complaint systems. In order to provide continuous monitoring, one needs multiple 'eyes' or auditors which are constantly available to monitor on-the-ground conditions. One way to achieve this is to involve workers and relevant stakeholders in the continuous monitoring of the workplace conditions through complaint systems. Complaint systems provide for 'second-order monitoring' (Barenberg, 2008) and strengthen the enforcement potential of VSS (Ascoly and Zeldenrust, 2003; Marx, 2014; Macdonald, 2019; ISEAL credibility principles[2]).

A fourth stream of research seeks to bring these elements together and looks at how different components of institutional design combine in the context of specific VSS or provide a comparative analysis of several VSS on their institutional design. (Marx, 2013; Fiorini et al., 2018; Collins et al., 2017; UNFSS, 2020). This line of

---

[2] http://www.isealalliance.org/our-work/defining-credibility/credibility-principles

research highlights five findings. First, there is significant variation in how VSS are designed. Second, most VSS have open and consensus-based standard-setting procedures, which involve several stakeholders. Third, many systems have open and consensus-based standard-setting procedures and third-party conformity assessment through auditing, but lack ex post verification tools such as complaint systems. Fourth, several VSS have open and consensus-based standard-setting procedures but no credible ex ante (auditing) and ex post (complaint-based systems) enforcement mechanisms. Finally, relatively few VSS have a well elaborated standard-setting and enforcement design. This diversity clearly shows that not all VSS are equal in terms of design and, ultimately, effectiveness.

3.3 EMERGENCE AND DRIVERS OF VSS ADOPTION

Marx and Wouters (2015) track the emergence of VSS and show that the seeds for VSS and the certification model can be traced back more than 100 years ago. However, the real take-off and proliferation of VSS is of much more recent nature (around the 1990s) and is triggered by distinct factors and pathways. Studies focusing on the emergence of VSS is sparked by many interrelated factors, and that the story about their emergence is partially different depending on the commodities covered and the type of VSS. These factors also constitute current drivers for VSS adoption. We identify five major drives for VSS adoption. Change in any of these drivers will influence adoption of VSS.

Consumer Demand

First of all, consumers have grown more conscious of sustainability issues and may adjust their purchasing behaviour in relation to the perceived sustainability of products (O'Rouke, 2012). VSS provide information, through the use of labels on the sustainability of products. This consumer consciousness has grown in stages. Early manifestations relate to the wish of consumers to address global inequality and empower local communities in developing countries. Fair Trade certificates are the prime example of VSS which emerged in response to this demand. Later on, with the emergence and 'mainstreaming' of sustainable development, consumer demand for sustainable products grew. This was also fuelled by increasing concerns on quality of mainly food products following many different food crises in Europe and United States in the 1990s (Ansell and Vogel, 2006). Consumers grew more conscious of food safety risks and adjusted their purchasing behaviour also as a function of the perceived reliability of food. As a consequence, supermarket chains and large producer groups have made food safety a key concern and a differentiating factor in the marketing of food products. For this market differentiation they use labels/certificates.

Brand Protection

Second, brand protection is a key issue for many leading companies. Changing strategies of NGOs, which directly targeted firms through the use of media campaigns and boycotts, have forced firms to take civil society concerns into account, and led them to engage with NGOs and set up VSS. This was especially true in the garment and textiles sectors. From the 1950s onwards, the apparel and footwear industry globalized at an impressive speed (Rosen, 2002). As a result, the industry became organized in global value chains and started outsourcing production to export-driven industrializing economies such as the Republic of Korea and Taiwan Province of China. In these production facilities workers often had to work under harsh conditions and labour rights were violated. This led, mainly from the 1980s onwards, to social protest in Europe. Coalitions such as the Clean Clothes Campaign emerged, effectively pressuring companies through public campaigning. Throughout the early 1990s, public awareness on the issue of labour rights also sharpened in the United States. In a long sequence of media reports (Bartley, 2003), business enterprises were directly targeted for not upholding labour standards throughout their value chain (Bartley, 2003, p. 443). They reacted quickly, initially by adopting codes of conduct in which they announced to address labour issues throughout the supply chain. However, instead of silencing protests, these actions generated more inquiry and confronted business enterprises with the fact that they were not living up to their code of conduct. NGOs were particularly distrusting corporations' self-

proclaimed adherence to codes of conduct, objecting that such initiatives were *"merely symbolic documents, completely detached from realities 'on the ground' in factories"* (Bartley, 2003, p. 445). Gereffi, Garcia-Johnson and Sasser note for example that protests and direct actions against brand-name retailers are only 15 years old, but are regarded as extremely powerful tools to force retailers to take environmental, social and safety issues into consideration (Gereffi et al., 2001, p. 64). Marx (2008) shows how brand-protection is a major factor in using VSS, especially for firms and brands who are publicly listed on a stock-exchange. The need to protect a brand resulted in increased consultations between business enterprises and several stakeholders and the emergence of multi-stakeholder platforms. For NGOs, this collaboration also offered benefits. Rather than being confrontational towards firms or try to influence firm behaviour via lobbying governments, NGOs are using a co-operative strategy towards firms of which VSS are prominent example. As long as VSS are considered to be a protection of a brand they will be adopted. Moreover, Van der Ven (2019) argues that the use of VSS by large consumer-oriented retailers actually influences the design and credibility of VSS since VSS targeting these firms specifically want to insulate these large forms from critical scrutiny.

Government Regulations

Thirdly, in some cases, government regulation has been and is a major driver of VSS development and adoption. As food markets, for example, became globalized and food products circulate extensively from one geographic zone to another the tracing of the origins of such products has become more difficult. Hence, it became more difficult for single governments to keep track of the range of products present on their domestic markets, and to keep up with the assessment of all the risks associated therewith. States therefore tended to place a kind of default responsibility on the food chain actors and required them to develop due diligence systems. An early example of such a due diligence requirement can be found in the United Kingdom Food Safety Act of 1990, which provides that food retailers can escape liability for non-compliance with food safety laws if they can demonstrate that they have taken all precautions in this regard. This liability provision arguably prompted a response from the food industry, resulting in the development of VSS (Henson and Humphrey, 2012). This early due diligence approach in the food sector is now spilling over to other sectors and with regard to issues of key importance for VSS such as the protection of human rights. This has led to the emergence and development of new Human Rights Due Diligence regulations which will impact producers all over the world (Bright et al., 2020). The importance of VSS for Human Rights Due Diligence is discussed by Partiti (2021) who analyses the effects of human rights due diligence on VSS. More in general, as the 4th UNFSS Flagship publication details, VSS are increasingly integrated in public policies, sometimes as conditions for market access, to enable governments to regulate 'behind their borders' or to operationalize a government's sustainability policy as is the case in sustainable public procurement (UNFSS, 2020).

Reaction to failure of multilateral efforts

Fourthly, VSS have emerged as a reaction to failure of multilateral efforts to address environmental issues such as the failure to reach a consensus on action to be taken to tackle deforestation. As Bartley (2011, p. 445) notes, "private efforts have also been perceived by many NGO's as a way to bypass political roadblocks". The Brundtland report 'Our Common Future' as well as 1992 United Nations Commission on Environment and Development (UNCED) summit in Rio de Janeiro identified deforestation as a key environmental issue. However, the UNCED summit failed to result in a binding commitment to address deforestation. As a result, private forest certification emerged as a tool to address sustainability issues related to forestry. The making and conceptualizing of forest certification pre-dates the UNCED conference (Bartley, 2007; Auld, 2014), but the conference triggered the further development of forest certification which then took off as one the key global governance tools for forest management (Cashore et al, 2004).

Reaction to other VSS

Fifthly, many VSS emerged as a reaction to other VSS. For example, NGO-driven VSS are sometimes countered by industry-driven VSS or vice versa, especially as different VSS often compete in the same markets.

This has resulted in the emergence of several VSS focusing on the same commodities. There has been some consolidation in terms of mergers between VSS but there also remains some dynamics in terms of new VSS emerging to certify commodities for which there are already other VSS available. Besides competition between different stakeholders in VSS (NGO versus industry VSS) there are also VSS emerging in different parts of the world which try to accommodate more local or regional sensitivities. However, overall, VSS remain more a developed countries phenomenon than a developing countries one (see Schleifer et al., 2020).

All these factors drive the development of the number of VSS as well as the adoption of specific VSS.

Box 4. VSS and Sustainable Development Goals

The 2030 Sustainable Development Goals provides a shared blueprint for peace and prosperity for people and the planet. VSS are discussed as a possible implementation mechanism for the 2030 Agenda (UNFSS, 2016). Beyond their direct relevance to SDG 12, (Responsible Consumption and Production), VSS would speak to a wide range of policy targets included in the SDGs, including food security, gender equality, climate action and many others. However, the empirical research in this area is still at a very early stage. On the one hand, there are those who see great potential for "credible" voluntary standard systems to play an important role in this area (WWF, 2017). Others, on the other hand, are less optimistic, pointing to shortcomings and limitations of VSS as a mode of sustainability governance (Bartley, 2010; Bennet, 2018).

Bissinger et al. (2020)find a significant overlap between voluntary sustainability standards (VSS) and the Sustainable Development Goals (SDGs). It showed that there is a large number of relevant VSS available for policy makers aiming to create synergies in the SDGs related areas.

Using data from the ITC Sustainability Map, a systematic analysis of the interlinkages between 232 VSS and the 17 SDGs and their targets is carried out. The result (see Figure 5) indicates that the three SDGs most widely covered by VSS are SDG 8 (Decent Work and Economic Growth), SDG 12 (Responsible Consumption and Production) and SDG 2 (Zero Hunger). There are more than 200 VSS linked with each of these goals. The standards are also relevant for other SDGs, with potential to enhance this relevance. These include SDG 16 (Peace, Justice and Strong Institutions), SDG 15 (Life on Land), SDG 5 (Gender Equality), SDG 9 (Industry, Innovation and Infrastructure), SDG 7 (Affordable and Clean Energy) and SDG 10 (Reduced Inequalities).

In summary VSS could contribute to the achievement of the SDGs by complementing the role of governments and international organizations. This is of a great value especially for developing countries in their attempt to move towards a sustainable future, better understand the SDGs and the implications of VSS.

Figure 5. Voluntary Standards linked to each SDG

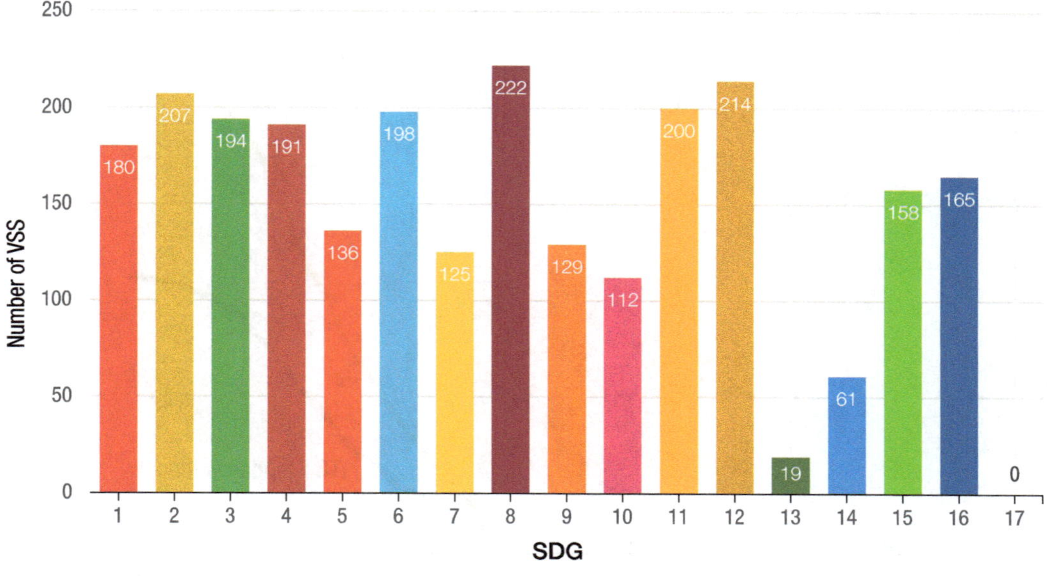

Source: Bissinger et al. (2020)

3.4 CHALLENGES OF VSS ADOPTION IN DEVELOPING COUNTRIES

There is quite some evidence that many developing countries face significant barriers of being integrated in VSS dynamics (Ponte, 2020; Renckens and Auld, 2019). The 4th UNFSS flagship publication (2020) provides a detailed analysis of the use of VSS across the world and shows that in terms of the use of the number of VSS as well as the use of specific VSS there is a developed-developing country divide. Some developing and middle-income countries are almost excluded from VSS dynamics (Marx and Cuypers, 2010; Marx & Wouters, 2017). Tayleur et al. (2018) find that certified entities are located in areas important for biodiversity conservation, but not in areas most in need for poverty alleviation and hence the poorest countries. Moreover, Schleifer, Fiorini and Fransen (2020) argue based on analysis of 47 VSS, covering 12 export oriented commodities, in the 10 largest developing countries that due to an highly unequal geographic and sectoral distribution, the lack of inclusion of producers in their central decision-making bodies, and the prevalence of problematic cost sharing arrangements limit the potential of VSS to contribute to sustainable commodity production in developing countries. Before we delve into some of the key barriers for VSS adoption we briefly introduce some key facts on the emergence, development and use of VSS.

The emergence, development and use of VSS

The importance of VSS can be measured by different indicators, such as the total number of VSS schemes that are active globally or in selected countries, the number of producers or firms that are certified, the number of certified hectares of production land, and the proportion of certified products per commodity.

The growth of VSS schemes can first be analysed by examining the evolution of their total number globally between 1940 and 2020 (Figure 6). Two VSS databases – the ITC Standards Map and the Ecolabel Index of the European Union – were used, which map out all existing VSS schemes and compile data on their requirements and procedures. The figure is based on the reported establishment date of VSS schemes, and only includes those that were still in existence.

Figure 6. **Evolution in the number of VSS active worldwide, 1940–2020**

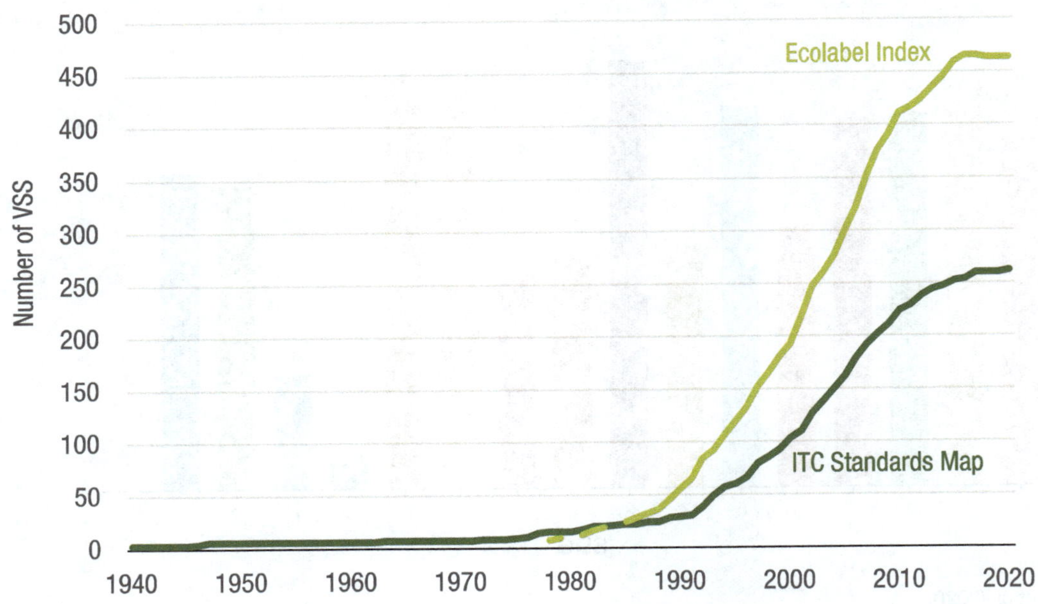

Source: UNFSS (2020).[3]

Despite the divergence in numbers between the ITC Standards Map and the Ecolabel Index,[4] two interesting trends can be discerned. First, although the idea of VSS is quite old (Marx and Wouters, 2015), their proliferation is more recent: VSS truly emerged in the 1990s, and their number grew consistently until the early 2010s. Second, growth in the number of active VSS has been slowing down in recent years, and has even stagnated since 2017, though it is unclear why this has happened.

However, the recent stagnation in the number of existing VSS schemes does not signify stagnation in their adoption by producers or firms along global value chains within different sectors which can be measured by the share of certified commodities in their respective markets. The *State of Sustainable Markets* annual reports of the ITC, in collaboration with the Research Institute of Organic Agriculture (FiBL) and the International Institute for Sustainable Development (IISD), have been providing the most comprehensive mapping and evolution of certified commodities globally since 2008. Those reports compile data from the 14 major VSS organizations[5] globally, covering 8 agricultural commodities – bananas, cocoa, coffee, cotton, palm oil, soybeans, sugarcane and tea – plus forestry. The main findings of the 2019 report show that certification has intensified over the past decade, in terms of both the proportion of certified commodities in their respective markets and the proportion of certified production area (Table 1).

---

[3] ITC (n.d.). ITC Standards Map. Available at: https://sustainabilitymap.org/standards?q=eyJzZWxlY3RlZENsaWVudCI6Ik5PIEFGRklMSUFUSU9OIn0%3D (accessed, March 2020); and Ecolabel Index (n.d.). Ecolabel Index. Available at: http://www.ecolabelindex.com/ecolabels/ (accessed, March 2020).

[4] This divergence is explained by different methodologies in the construction of the databases. The ITC Standards Map is typically more restrictive, as it relies on data quality review from independent experts as well as from standards organizations themselves. The Ecolabel Index is more comprehensive, as it aims to map out all existing VSS schemes without review requirements. Hereinafter, data from the ITC Standards Map is used.

[5] The 14 VSS organizations are: 4C Services (4C), Better Cotton Initiative (BCI), Bonsucro, Cotton made in Africa (CmiA), Fairtrade International (Fairtrade), Forest Stewardship Council (FSC), GLOBALG.A.P., IFOAM – Organics International (organic), Programme for the Endorsement of Forest Certification (PEFC), ProTerra Foundation (ProTerra), Rainforest Alliance (Rainforest), Roundtable on Sustainable Palm Oil (RSPO), Round Table on Responsible Soy (RTRS) and UTZ (a programme and certification scheme for sustainable farming).

Table 1. Evolution of certification in selected agricultural commodities and forestry

Commodity	Share of certified production volume in total production, 2017 (Per cent)	Growth in share of certified production volume in total production, 2013-2017 (Per cent)	Share of certified production land in total production land, 2017 (Per cent)	Growth in share of certified production land in total production land, 2013-2017 (Per cent)
Bananas	5.6	+88.7	6.0	+28.6
Cocoa	29.4	+58.2	24.8	+114.7
Coffee	26.1	-7.8	23.4	+8.7
Cotton	NA	NA	16.2	+172.4
Palm oil	NA	NA	11.9	+26.1
Soybeans	1.5	+34.3	1.5	-5.9
Sugarcane	NA	NA	7.6	+80.2
Tea	20.9	+71.0	16.4	+77.3
Forestry	NA	NA	10.8	+27.9[a]

Source: Willer et al. (2019).

[a] For wood, the reference period is 2010–2017

NA = data not available

In addition, the report estimates that the area of production land certified by the 12 leading agricultural VSS under study accounts for only 1.94 per cent of total agricultural land area globally (Willer et al., 2019: 7), but that this percentage is increasing. This increase is confirmed by Tayleur et al. (2017), who mapped out the coverage of 12 major agricultural VSS,[6] and found that certified cropland is growing by approximately 11 per cent a year. However, similar to the findings of the *State of Sustainable Markets 2019* report, the authors also show that only 1.1 per cent of global cropland is certified by those 12 major VSS.

While the proportion of land under certified production globally remains limited, it is nonetheless growing, and certified products are gaining market shares as well. However, this trend is not uniform across all countries. Tayleur et al. (2017) analysed the proportion of land under certified production by country. They showed that certification is more intensive in some countries than in others. Countries scoring high (> 10 per cent of production land certified) include Austria, Belize, Colombia, Costa Rica, Côte d'Ivoire, Dominican Republic (the), Guatemala, Italy, Malaysia, Papua New Guinea, Peru, Sierra Leone, Sweden and Zambia. Other countries, such as Brazil, El Salvador, Estonia, Ghana, Honduras, Indonesia, Kenya, Latvia, Lithuania, Mexico, Nicaragua and Spain also score relatively high (> 5 per cent).

Another way to approach the significance of VSS is too look how active they are across the globe. Based on data from the ITC Standards Map, the degree of VSS adoption of a given country is measured as the percentage of active VSS in that country in relation to the total number of active VSS worldwide. Figure 7 provides an overview of countries in which VSS are active and how VSS-intensive these countries are. The darker the colour the more VSS are active in that country.

---

[6] Namely: 4C Services (4C), Better Cotton Initiative (BCI), Bonsucro, Cotton made in Africa (CmiA), Fairtrade International (Fairtrade), GLOBALG.A.P., IFOAM – Organics International (organic), ProTerra Foundation (ProTerra), Rainforest Alliance (Rainforest), Roundtable on Sustainable Palm Oil (RSPO), Round Table on Responsible Soy (RTRS), Roundtable on Sustainable Biomaterials, and UTZ.

Figure 7. VSS adoption intensity map per country (as a percentage of all VSS)

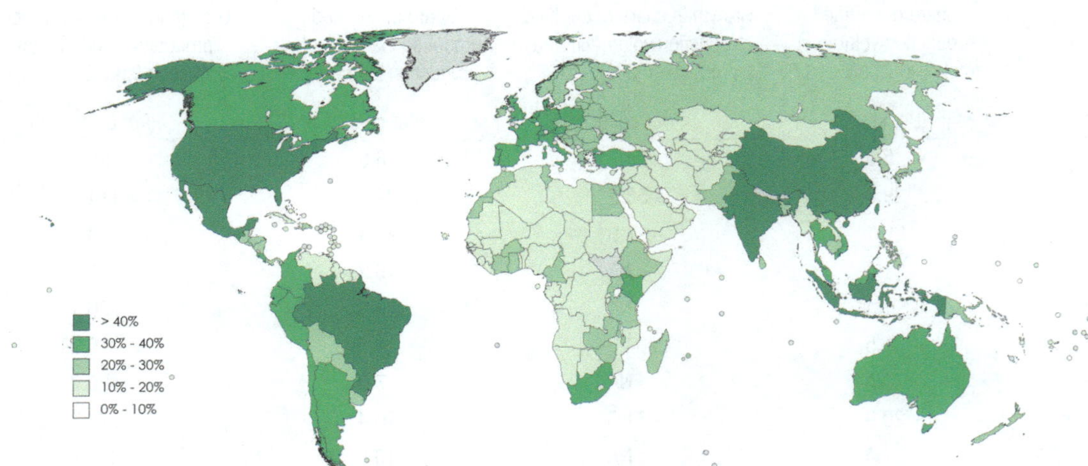

Source: UNFSS (2020).[7]

Five observations can be made from an analysis of the distribution of VSS across countries (UNFSS, 2020). First, it appears that VSS are found in all countries,[8] but that there is considerable variation between countries, which can be expected on the basis of the size of the economy. Brazil, China, India, Indonesia, Mexico the United States of America, for example, are leading in VSS use. Second, variation in use scores appears to more or less align with income levels. Indeed, low-income countries – and, to some extent, lower-middle-income countries – feature low in the table, meaning that low-income countries tend to count fewer VSS than high- or upper- middle-income countries. Nonetheless, and as a third observation, variation in adoption scores does not perfectly align with income level. Japan, for example, despite being the third largest economy in the world, only ranks 35th in the VSS adoption score, after Honduras and Sri Lanka. The Russian Federation , as the 12th largest economy in the world, ranks only 62nd. The size or income level of an economy is therefore not the only determinant of the extent of VSS adoption within a country. More so, and fourth, some lower-middle-income countries score high, such as Viet Nam (10th position), Indonesia (5th position) and India (4th position). Income level therefore does not necessarily predict the VSS adoption ranking. Rather, the well-scoring lower-middle-income countries are typically countries that pursue an export-oriented industrialization policy. Lastly, even some low-income countries score fairly high, such as the United Republic of Tanzania, as aforementioned, and Ethiopia (37th) – just below Japan and above Sweden. It is worth noting that these low-income countries that score relatively high export commodities, such as coffee, which can be certified by multiple certificates.

Barriers to VSS Adoption

What are some of the main challenges for VSS use in developing countries? Throughout the literature one can identify several barriers. A first barrier is constituted by the costs involved in receiving certification. A second barrier relates to a lack of incentives. A third barrier results from a governance gap. A final barrier refers to political dynamics and possible opposition towards VSS.

Barrier related to costs to obtain certification

A first major hurdle relates to the costs involved in getting certified (Auld and Renckens, 2021; Carter, Scott and Mahallati, 2018; Marx and Cuyers, 2010). Obtaining VSS can be costly, especially when producers

---

[7] ITC (n.d.). ITC Standards Map. Available at: https://sustainabilitymap.org/standards?q=eyJzZWxlY3RlZENsaWVudCl6lk5PlEFGRklMSUFUSU9Oln0%3D (accessed, March 2020).

[8] The ITC Standards Map does not provide data for Liechtenstein, Monaco, San Marino and South Sudan. While those countries do, nonetheless, count a few VSS active on their territory, they are excluded from our analysis.

need to undertake major changes in day-to-day management practices in order to comply with standards and requirements. The costs of certification are a function of size, complexity, and whether first-time certification or re-certification is concerned. First-time certification is often substantially more expensive because it often requires an extensive certification process that, in general, consists of several steps. First, the applicant invites an inspector, who conducts a pre-audit or feasibility study on whether the entity under consideration can be certified. This pre-audit is data and time intensive and often involves the making of management plans which outline how the entity will comply with the standards. Therefore, the applicant needs to provide data on all relevant standards. These data are often not readily available, especially in developing countries. Second, a genuine audit is conducted, which assesses the management of the entity against the standards and criteria. This audit also contains detailed non-compliances (NCs) and corrective actions requests (CARs) that are necessary to achieve certification. The third step involves implementing the corrective actions as well as an assessment of the audit by the applicant. Step four is a new audit, which often contains further corrective actions that need to be implemented. Step five finalizes the process by awarding the certificate for a number of years.

One of the major bottlenecks between steps two and five is the lack of technical knowledge to address major deficiencies. The auditor does not play the role of a consultant and audits typically do not contain information on how non-compliances should be addressed. These roles are strictly divided to prevent any conflict of interest. In other words, the auditor points to the deficiencies that need to be addressed by corrective actions, but does not say *how* they can be addressed. Hence, producers interested in certification often have to invest additionally to obtain this technical expertise. Consequently, first-time certification (i) requires an upfront investment that can be expensive (audit fees, corrective actions, etc.), and (ii) requires technical and informational expertise which need to be hired in order comply. Besides the costs of achieving certification there are also costs related to changed production process to adhere to the standards.

The effort and resources required to carry out these tasks inhibit the adoption of VSS. Hence, costs are an important barrier for VSS adoption and hence initial financial as well as technical support is key to the inclusion of target producer groups within export value chains. As the FAO report highlights *"smallholders need to be organized in commercially viable arrangement to be able to participate in certified value chains"*. (Loconto and Dankers, 2014, p. ix, see also pp. 59-60).

Related, since it might increase adjustment costs, some authors point to the fact that participation of developing countries is hindered by the fact that VSS rely to a degree on Western sustainability standards and data requirements for audits which are hard to comply with for producers in developing countries (Auld & Renckens, 2021; Ponte, 2008; Stratoudakis et al., 2016). This also significantly increases costs. Producers used to work with auditing and verification procedures much more easily adjust to procedures used by VSS.

Barrier related to lack of incentives to obtain certification

The costs incurred to obtain certification need, to a degree, be covered by additional revenue. In other words, there needs to be a return on investment. This is not to argue that producers only engage in VSS certification because of economic reasons. Other social and cultural reasons might determine the choice for certification or more sustainable production processes. However, economic return provides an important incentive of becoming certified for producers. This incentive can take two forms; either through a price premium or access to (export) markets. When expected economic impacts are uncertain incentives for VSS use decrease (Auld & Renckens, 2021; Grabs, 2020).

Price premium. in some cases, a price (or income) premium is an institutionalized component of the VSS as is the case with Fair Trade VSS (Naegele, 2020). Such an approach can lead to direct additional income for producers, but depends to a degree on the willingness of consumers to pay higher prices. In other words, an expected revenue can emerge from the fact that certified products are sold at a higher price and that this windfall trickles down to the producers. However, concerning the latter there is not much evidence of a strong income effect through higher prices for certified goods. This can be explained by different dynamics. First, there is no strong evidence that there is a willingness to pay significantly higher prices for certified good by consumers

(Hiscox et al., 2015). There are some consumers who are willing to pay a higher price for certified goods, but not that many. There is a demand for certified goods and consumers will consciously choose for certified goods if the price remains the same. Second, there is some evidence that in cases when consumers do pay a higher price for certified goods, this higher price does not necessarily trickles down the value chain to the producers. Often intermediate actors in the value chain capture the gains (Ruerd, 2008; Ruerd et al., 2009) Third, important buyers of certified goods are not consumers but other businesses. They buy certified goods for multiple reasons, but not necessarily to include them in products which then are sold for higher prices (Vlosky and Aguilar, 2007). As a result, they are not willing to pay higher prices for certified products. Certification becomes a condition to be able to sell to certain buyers (see next point).

Access to (export) markets. A second important incentive concerns the access to markets VSS might provide. VSS can act as facilitators to trade but also as barriers to trade. The latter was made clear by a well-known example which reached the World Trade Organisation when banana producers from a small Caribbean Islands group St Vincent and Grenadines were confronted with certification requirements from mainly supermarkets in the United Kingdom. They were not able to obtain certification because of the costs involved and were no longer able to access the European retailer market. Quite suddenly they lost their export markets to other banana producers (Stanton, 2012). Through making adherence to VSS compulsory for entering markets VSS can generate access-to-market problems and decrease the export share for producers who do not want or are unable to comply (Loconto and Dankers, 2014). To the contrary, VSS can also be a catalyst to trade for those who do adhere to VSS and hence open up export markets. The degree to which this incentive plays out will depend on the degree developing countries export VSS relevant products (not for all products are VSS available) and where they export to. If export remains limited in general and limited to (surrounding) markets with limited demand for VSS labelled products the incentives to certify will remain low. However, it should be noted that the above should not be interpreted that there is no demand for certified products in developing countries. In an interesting case study on South-South trade with regard to tea Bloomfield (2020) shows that there is a demand for sustainable products in developing countries. He analyzes the Ceylon tea industry and shows that despite it is exporting most of its tea to Southern markets it is also one of the leaders in terms of economic, social and environmental practices.

Barrier related to weak governance institutions (governance gap)

Several studies have started to highlight the importance of the political and institutional context in which VSS are being used pointing to the possible importance of governance gaps for VSS adoption. In a case study of Indonesia, Bartley (2014, 2019) argues that understanding the political context of a country is important for understanding the dynamics of forest certification practice. Similarly, a recent literature review of more than 100 studies argued that a necessary but insufficient condition for the use of VSS is national institutions which provide a supporting environment for compliance with standards and regulatory compliance (Loconto and Dankers, 2014, p. 9). Locke et al. (2009, see also Lock, 2013), in analyzing Nike's supply chain (which sources from many different counties), found that compliance with labour standards as measured by factory audits was higher in countries with a higher level of rule of law and regulatory capacity.

The idea is that countries which have developed effective and well-functioning governance structures constitute a better institutional context for the use of VSS. In other words, countries which score well on good governance indicators are hypothesized to have higher degrees of VSS use. The operationalization of what exactly is understood under political institutional context and governance structure remains quite vague but it is clear that in countries where there in general is more rule-compliance the likelihood of the use of VSS increases. Marx and Wouters (2017), who analyzed the relationship between governance indicators and the occurrence of VSS, show that VSS are more widely used in countries which already have a strong and effective regulatory government system. Entities based in these countries are probably more used to comply with (public/ mandatory) standards and rules. Hence, the 'governance gap' they need to close in order to conform with VSS standards is much less in comparison with those entities situated in countries with weaker regulatory state (i.e., governance structure).

The importance of this 'governance fit' is also substantiated by some case studies. Basso et al. (2011, see also Basso et al. 2012) for example analyzed the degree to which certified entities (forest units) complied with existing national environmental and labour legislation. They found still some non-compliances which were related to environmental and labour legislation. However, they noted that the certification process did spot these non-compliances and required corrective actions in order to maintain certification. Hence, the authors concluded that certification contributes to the further enforcement of existing national legislation in forest management units of plantation. The case study also shows that being already more or less aligned and acquainted with complying with rules facilitates the certification process. In other words, certification is facilitated if certified entities are used to comply with rules and this is typically more the case in countries with strong regulatory and compliance systems. Moreover, as von Essen and Lambin (2021) argue the 'governance fit' is also important for the effectiveness on the ground of VSS since producers seeking certification often depend on '*supporting policies and enabling conditions created by local public authorities, such as law enforcement, clear land property rights and support for marginal producers.*' (p. 2; see also Lambin and Thorlakson, 2018)

On the other hand, from a trade perspective, some studies proposed that VSS can work as a tool to bridge the governance gap between countries. The idea is that adopting VSS will lead to strengthening existing institutions and make them more effective. This in turn will lead to the further enhancement of trade. Fiankor et al. (2019) illustrate this empirically by analyzing the effects of GlobalGAP certification measured on country level on the 'governance quality' of a country (measured by the World Bank Governance Indicators) and trade.

Barrier related to socio-political resistance to VSS

Some authors also identify political resistance as a barrier for VSS adoption. They report that VSS are sometimes viewed as mechanisms that enforce existing power relations, especially by lead firms in global value chains which are often located in developed countries. These firms define sustainability according to their perspective and interests and apply this approach to all suppliers which can generate resistance to the use of VSS (Auld and Renckens, 2021, p. 3; Levy, Reinecke and Manning, 2016). This re-enforcing of existing power relations might lead to asymmetric adoption dynamics in developing countries which favour large economic operators over small-scale community-based operations, has been described in several case studies (see for example Pinto and McDermott 2013; Klooster, 2005). It might also further intensify developing and developed countries imbalances in VSS dynamics because firms in developed countries are more experienced in complying with such (developed) countries standards or because governments provide financial assistance to their domestic operators to comply (Renckens and Auld, 2019).

This developed, developing countries tension or divide might lead to disincentives to certify. Starobin (2020), for example, describes the phenomenon of uncertified producers in Nicaragua, of otherwise certifiable organic food embedded in value chains whose farm products conform to elevated environmental standards. According to how they produce commodities these producers would be eligible for certification. However, they remain either unable (because of costs involved) but also unwilling (because of political resistance reasons) to obtain certification. She shows how, as a reaction to certification, these producers advance alternative, more localized, institutional arrangements.

The developing countries reactions to developed countries standards is also emphasized in other studies focusing on the standard-setting process both in terms of the substance of standards as well as with regard to who is involved in standard-setting processes. Some scholars are critical in this respect and emphasize the limited involvement of local producers in standard-setting processes (Bennett, 2017; Schouten & Bitzer, 2015).

This resistance to VSS can come from individual producers but it can also come from governments in developing countries. In some cases, governments support obtaining VSS which can lead to adoption of VSS. However, sometimes government support is reversed for economic or political reasons and adoption of VSS decreases or disappears) (Espinoza & Dockry, 2014).

4. VSS IMPACT AND EFFECTIVENESS

International trade is an enabler for sustainable development. International trade can create jobs, stimulate innovation and increase wealth and well-being (see Box 1). Especially for developing countries, expanding integration into GVCs is an opportunity for inclusive economic growth. Nevertheless, international trade may also lead to goal conflicts and/or difficult tradeoffs between individual SDGs. Producers from developing countries are often located at the beginning of GVCs, which provide primary goods and raw materials for more advanced, knowledge intensive and profitable intermediate production steps in developed countries.[9] While lead firms from developed countries reap high profits, producers from developing countries often earn barely enough to cover production costs (Dietz et al. 2020). This highly unequal profit sharing may also have adverse effects on labour rights, as producers in developing countries have limited financial leverage to improve social conditions, such as the payment of living wages. Moreover, production sites in developing countries are home to some of the most valuable ecological habitats on earth, including highly biodiverse rainforests or coastal waters. Intensified global demand and trade provides incentives to expand production into many of these habitats, which in turn may result in severe and irreversible environmental damages.

The effects of VSS on improving trade for sustainable development predominately depends on their capacity to effectively address pressing issues of economic, social and environmental sustainability along global GVCs. Stated plainly, the impact of VSS on sustainability outcomes hinges on two key factors: adoption effectiveness and on-site-effectiveness. As explained above, VSS are not mandated through law but depend on voluntary adoption. Without voluntary adoption, VSS cannot produce tangible effects. However, adoption alone is not sufficient. After adoption, real changes towards sustainable practices on the ground at production sites must follow. Like public policies, VSS may experience gaps between what they assume will be the effects of adopting their standards on paper, and what actually happens in practice. One important question is, therefore, to what extent VSS are capable, after adoption, of achieving their goals of improving the economic, social and environmental performance of certified production sites — especially in developing countries.

A sizeable body of literature has developed in recent decades to assess the on-site effects of certified production sites, which, since the 2000s, has grown rapidly. Researches in industrial relations have interrogated whether VSS have an impact on labour relations (Locke 2013; Locke and Romis 2010). Development researchers have investigated the socio-economic effects of VSS on poverty reduction (Cramer et al. 2017; Dietz et al. 2020), Scholars of land-use governance have analyzed the effects of VSS on deforestation rates (Garrett et al. 2021; Lambin et al. 2014), economists have assessed the impacts of VSS on productivity (Kilian et al. 2004; Kilian et al. 2006) and ecologists have examined whether VSS help restore natural habitats and safeguard biodiversity (Blumroeder et al. 2019). VSS research therefore cuts across the social and natural sciences, and scholars have utilized a wide range of different research designs to explore their performance on the ground.

Existing meta-studies reviewing this literature are few and highly fragmented. Most focus on select — or even single — VSS (Cattau et al. 2016; Carlson and Palmer 2016; Bouslah et al. 2010; DeFries et al. 2017; Froese and Proelss 2012; Parkes et al. 2010). Other studies summarize the literature on selected environmental (Garrett et al. 2016; Burivalova et al. 2017), social or economic (Blackman and Rivera 2011; Sellare et al. 2020) outcome variables (e.g. de-forestation rates, price premiums, worker empowerment). Unsurprisingly, the results are as diverse as the disciplines assessing them, and the landscapes they govern, with scholars finding both positive and negative outcomes of VSS utilization.

Nevertheless, developing a clear picture of how well VSS are collectively facilitating a transition to more sustainable production practices is critical. Thus, the main aim of this chapter is to provide a structured overview of the literature to date that has assessed the on-site effectiveness of VSS. To this end, we start by providing a stylized version of the theory of change which underpins the work of VSS. In their theories of change, VSS define

---

[9] The situation is different for emgering market economies especially in Asia which are also largely involved in more knowledge intense intermediate production steps.

the causal steps (impact pathways) which, they theorize, lead from standard development to tangible changes towards more sustainable modes production at the ground level of certified production sites.

4.1 IMPACT PATHWAYS

In order to promote changes towards more sustainable modes of trade and production, VSS begin by setting up sustainability standards that define how different economic actors along global value chains ought to behave (Dietz et al. 2018). Most importantly, these standards contain economic, environmental and social regulations that control the production and trade of standard compliant products: In detail, VSS define the following sets of regulatory standards:

- *Economic regulations* (e.g. price regulations), which regulate the conditions under which downstream value chain actors can trade standard compliant products along GVCs down to the level of retailers.

- *Environmental regulations*, which place limits and prohibitions on resource extraction (e.g. prohibitions on clearing primary forest, obligations to respect fish catch quotas), dictate permissible and prohibited inputs (e.g. banning or reducing the use of certain chemicals or genetically modified organisms), specify requirements for disposal of waste materials (e.g. wastewater treatment or plastics collection and recycling), and teach producers to safeguard essential ecosystem services (e.g. preventing topsoil erosion).

- *Social regulations and labour standards* (e.g. obligations to respect Indigenous People's rights or provide protective equipment to workers), which regulate behaviour at the producer level.

In addition, VSS may include standards that do not focus on the regulatory control but the empowerment of certified producers. Such standards require greater commitments and more collaboration by downstream value chain actors. In detail, these standards include:

- *Capacity building standards* (e.g. obligations to train producers in good agricultural practices) which regulate the provision of trainings events to certified producers through management entities or certification holders (e.g. traders), who often organize one or several groups of certified producers.
- *Awareness raising standards* (obligation to provide opportunities for women to facilitate empowerment), which regulate the provision of awareness-raising events to certified producers.

The success of VSS depends on the rise of a critical mass of standard compliant markets (from producers to consumers) incentivizing economic actors to adopt their standard systems (Cashore et al. 2004; Büthe 2010; Vogel 2008). Under such conditions, value chain actors on all levels are expected to voluntarily agree to certification in order to access standard compliant markets (*standard adoption*). After adoption, VSS monitor compliance through third-party audits (Dietz et al. 2018). Through de-certification, they can also sanction those producers who violate their requirements and exclude them from standard compliant markets (Grabs 2020). In doing so, VSS intend to ensure that subsequent to standard adoption, value chain actors implement the sustainability standards and change their production practices accordingly.

With adoption, the different types of standards mentioned above (environmental and social regulations, capacity-building and awareness raising standards and economic standards) transform into interventions that, according to VSSs' theories of change, may drive substantial behavioural changes which in turn should correspond with a number of different intermediate and end-point sustainability outcomes (Oya et al. 2018). In detail, VSS create five different types of interventions, each of which intend to improve the sustainability performance of certified production sites along a distinct impact pathway.

- *Market interventions*: Upon standard adoption, downstream value chain actors grant preferable economic conditions to standard compliant producers (e.g. price premiums are paid). As a consequence, economic conditions for producers improve (e.g. producers receive higher prices), which in turn are

expected to increase household incomes and producer well-being. Moreover, market interventions are assumed to provide the incentives necessary for producers to adopt and comply with VSS.

- ***Regulatory interventions***: Upon standard adoption, participants must invest in their production practices to comply with basic human and labour rights as well as environmental standards (e.g. primary forests are not cut, protective gear is provided to workers). Producers improve their environmental and social practices (e.g. wastewater is treated, harsh chemical inputs are avoided, child labour is eliminated), which in turn is expected to improve environmental and social sustainability outcomes (e.g. reduced effluent runoff in critical watersheds, better educational outcomes for children and youth).

- ***Capacity building interventions***: Upon standard adoption, managing entities/certifications holders begin to conduct capacity-building events (e.g. producers are trained in GAP and/or professional management skills). As a consequence, productivity rises (e.g. technical training that leads to increased yields). Thus, capacity building can also ultimately be associated with improved economic and social sustainability (higher household income, increased involvement of women in decision-making).

- ***Awareness raising interventions***: Upon standard adoption, management entities/certification holders begin to conduct awareness raising events (e.g. awareness raising events on women's empowerment are conducted). As a consequence, awareness on critical social issues (such as women being disempowered) increases, which in turn is expected to lead to improved social behaviour and sustainability outcomes (e.g. women's increasing agency).

4.2 POTENTIAL EFFECTS AND IMPACTS OF VSS ON IMPROVING TRADE FOR SUSTAINABLE DEVELOPMENT

Of course, this summary of the different interventions is highly simplified. However, usually VSS combine some or several of these interventions to promote sustainable changes. In detail, given the four types of interventions we outlined above, we see three major impacts of how VSS may improve trade relations, thereby fostering sustainable development.

I. *Improving profit and power sharing between lead firms from developed countries and producers of primary goods in developing countries (economic sustainability):* Producers from developing countries are often located at the beginning of GVCs, providing primary goods and raw material for more advanced, knowledge intense and profitable intermediate production steps in developed countries. While lead firms from developed countries are often able to capture the large majority of the benefits of these business relations, producers from developing countries sometimes earn barely enough to cover production costs. VSS aim to address this issue of economic sustainability in two ways. First, through market interventions that require downstream value chain actors to pay price premiums for standard compliant products, VSS ought to facilitate more egalitarian forms of profit-sharing within GVCs. Second, VSS may increase the profits of certified producers through the organization of trainings that teach certified producers to increase the quality of their goods and productivity of their production sites. With both types of interventions, VSS intend to increase the incomes and well-being of certified producers (economic sustainability).

II. *Reconciling international trade with environmental sustainability goals (environmental sustainability):* Functioning markets are fundamental to economic development. However, functioning ecosystems are foundational to functional markets. Thus, trade must be embedded in public laws and regulations that address the environmental consequences of production to ensure the ongoing stability of GVCs. If business actors can dispose freely of their waste in the environment, without paying for it, the consequences of pollution are not taken into account (traditionally described by economists as negative externalities) when making decisions about production and trade. Thus, production decisions that appear rational in the short-term can even undermine the ability of those businesses to continue producing in the medium- and long-term. Current efforts to achieve the socioeconomic SDGs by 2030 through increased trade

may thus also increase the human ecological footprint and intensify the pressure on already-exceeded planetary boundaries. In the context of international trade and GVCs, it is a fundamental problem that territorially organized national legal systems are hardly able to effectively regulate transborder business conduct. Lead firms often take advantage of these regulatory gaps by outsourcing production steps to regions with less strict environmental laws, while national governments, in turn, are disincentivized from ratifying stringent environmental or labour protections for fear of losing important trade relationships. Given their non-state market-based character, VSS have widely been regarded as one possible solution to re-embed global trade and production practices into a system of environmental norms that, unlike national legislation, can travel through and operate within the infrastructure of GVCs. With their environmental regulatory interventions (see above), VSS may have a positive impact on improving trade for sustainable development by creating a new mechanism that reduces negative environmental externalities, especially in regions with weaker state-based regulatory environments.

III. Reconciling international trade with basic human and labour rights (social sustainability): Also, workers — especially those in developing countries — can benefit tremendously from international trade. Because trade raises the amount that an economy can produce by letting firms and workers play to their comparative advantage, trade should also cause the average level of wages in an economy to rise. However, workers in many low-income countries around the world also work under conditions that violate basic human labour rights. The range of these legal violations ranges from unfairly garnished or withheld wages and unsafe working environments, to worst case scenarios, where production may involve the labour of small children or workers who are treated like twenty-first century slaves. A further pressing issue concerns the role of women and gender equality in GVCs.[10]

Most VSS have incorporated central international labour and human rights standards into their standard catalogues and certification processes. With their social regulatory interventions (see above) VSS are therefore widely regarded as a new regulatory tool with the potential to improve pressing labour and human rights issues in international trade and production.

All in all, we can conclude that VSS take a holistic approach to sustainable development that aims to improve the economic, environmental and social sustainability of international trade and production. From a policy perspective that aims to improve and foster more sustainable trade relations, especially between developing and developed counties, the pivotal issue is to assess the extent to which VSS indeed reach these goals.

4.3 ASSESSING THE EFFECTS AND IMPACTS ON VSS ON BETTER TRADE FOR SUSTAINABLE DEVELOPMENT

The TRANS SUSTAIN Project[11] at the University of Münster has recently developed a literature base with 176 scholarly, peer reviewed articles published between 2000 and 2020 that have empirically investigated the ground-level effects of VSS on more sustainable modes of production and trade.[12] The literature database has been utilized to review the existing state of the knowledge on VSS in order to provide systematic, evidence-based answers to the following three questions:

- To what extent do VSS improve the profits and economic well-being of certified producers (***economic sustainability***)?

- To what extent do VSS catalyze the implementation of improved environmental standards that reduce the ecological footprint of production and increase on-site biodiversity (***environmental sustainability***)?

---

[10] See: https://unctad.org/topic/gender-equality).

[11] The TRANS SUSTAIN Project is funded by the Ministry of Culture and Science of North Rhine-Westphalia, Germany.

[12] In the annex we lay out in detail, how the literature has been selected and which VSS are covered.

- To what extent do VSS assure the implementation of basic human and labour rights that improve the livelihoods of workers at certified production sites (***social sustainability***).

Since the literature TRANS SUSTAIN included in the literature database is highly heterogeneous (in that it includes both qualitative and quantitative as well experimental and non-experimental study designs), it was not possible to identify a straightforward common empirical denominator on the basis of which such diverse research could be easily compared. However, independent of the specific type of article, all articles in the literature base have in common that, subsequent to their empirical analyses, they interpret, summarize and evaluate their results on the on-site effects of VSS in conclusive statements. Such final evaluations are usually part of the discussion and/or conclusion section of an article. TRANS SUSTAIN focused on these final evaluative statements as the common unit of analysis in order to synthesize the pertinent literature and interpret these evaluative statements according to the following coding system: code 1 if an article concludes with a largely positive statement about the on-site effectiveness of VSS; code 2 if an article concludes with a mixed statement; code 3 if an article concludes with a largely negative evaluative statement (this includes both evaluations stating that VSS had either no or negative effects).

Overview

In order to produce a general overview, TRANS SUSTAIN calculated the distribution of positive, mixed and negative evaluations across all 176 articles. Figure 8 summarizes the results of this analysis in visual form. The results draw an unconvincing picture of the capability of VSS to increase sustainability outcomes at certified production sites. As becomes clear from Figure 8 many of the 176 articles (42.6 per cent) conclude with negative evaluations of the capability of VSS to make production and trade more sustainable, followed by mixed evaluations with a share of 33 per cent. Positive evaluations were only found for 24.4 per cent of the reviewed papers.

Figure 8. **Capabilities of VSS to increase sustainability outcomes in available literature**

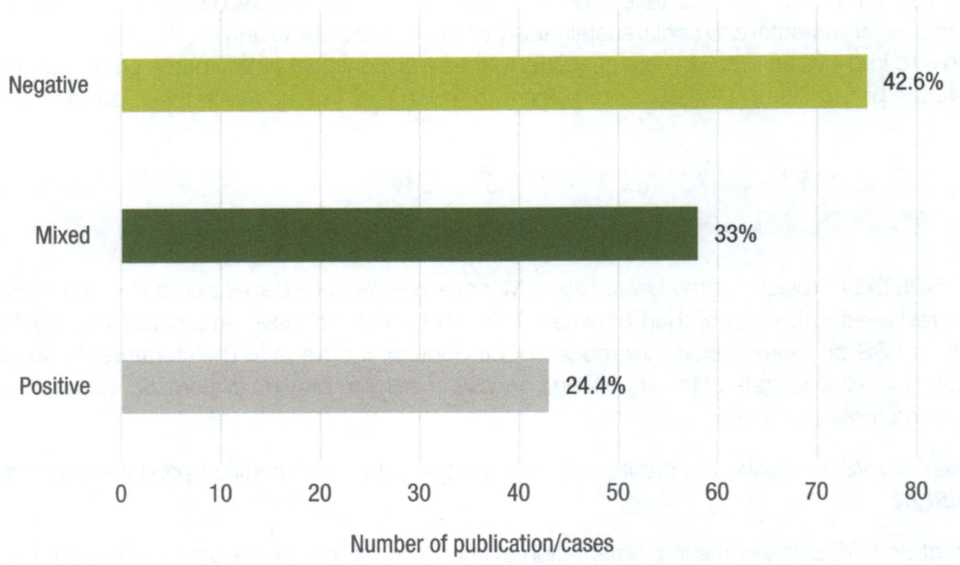

Economic, social and environmental sustainability

The literature database distinguishes the articles further according to the area of sustainability they address. As outlined above, studies that address issues of economic sustainability mostly analyze the implementation of price regulations (price premiums) and productivity trainings through VSS. Many also interpret the effects that these interventions have had on the household incomes and well-being of certified producers, with the focus on poverty reduction in developing countries. All in all, TRANS SUSTAIN identified 150 cases among the 176 articles in the literature database that have evaluated the effects of VSS on economic sustainability outcome variables. In 41 per cent of these cases, these evaluations have been negative, followed by a nearly even split between mixed evaluations (29 per cent) and positive evaluations (31 per cent).

Articles focusing on environmental sustainability typically focus on the implementation of environmental standards, such as prohibitions to cut forests, obligations to respect fish catch quotas, or bans of the most hazardous agro-chemicals. Some also assess the impacts of these standards on reducing ecological footprints and improving biodiversity on or near certified production sites. TRANS SUSTAIN has identified 151 cases in the pertinent literature that have evaluated the effects of VSS on such environmental outcome variables. Similar to outcomes from economic evaluations, the picture is even slightly more dominated by negative evaluations (44 per cent), indicating that VSS either did not or even exacerbated negative effects on the ecological footprint and biodiversity of certified production sites. Positive evaluations could only be found in 27 per cent of the cases, while mixed results show a rate of 30 per cent.

Finally, studies that deal with issues of social sustainability typically focus on the implementation of basic human and labour rights, such as prohibitions on forced labour (including child labour prohibitions or the provision of channels to safely address sexual harassment), the payment of living wages and the impacts of such standards on work safety, health and livelihood conditions as well as the empowerment of disempowered groups and individuals. TRANS SUSTAIN has identified 127 cases in which the pertinent literature has evaluated the effects of VSS on social outcomes variables. Interestingly, the pertinent literature evaluates the impacts of VSS on social sustainability issues more positively than for economic and environmental sustainability outcomes. For cases that study social outcome variables, many (39 per cent) include a positive evaluation, followed by negative assessments (35 per cent) and mixed results (26 per cent). Overall, Figure 9 therefore indicates that VSS may be more successful in reaching their social goals than their economic and/or environmental goals.

Figure 9. Capabilities of VSS to increase social, environmental and economic sustainability outcomes in available literature

Impact of VSS on Intermediate and endpoint sustainability outcomes

The concept of intermediate vs. endpoint variables helps us to add further nuance to this picture of the sustainability effects of VSS on global production and trade (Oya et al. 2018). Technically speaking, intermediate sustainability outcomes present pathway variables that are theorized to lead to the achievement of higher-level sustainability goals (endpoint outcomes).

Take for example, in the area of economic sustainability, the variable of price premiums paid to producers of standard compliant products. Researchers interested in studying the economic impacts of VSS may well discover that certified producers are paid higher wages than conventional producers for their certified coffee, cacao, fish, timber or whatever good it is that they sell (Fayet und Vermeulen 2014). Based on these findings, they may conclude that VSS are indeed successful in improving the economic conditions of certified producers. However, other studies found out that these price premiums (intermediate outcome) failed to translate into economic endpoint outcomes such higher household incomes for smallholders and waged workers, nor did they increase well-being (Oya et al 2018). For example, the additional revenues that producers generate through price premiums can ultimately be too modest to cover the costs of certification and associated on-site investments to meet VSS requirements (Dietz und Grabs 2021).

A further example to illustrate the conceptual difference between intermediate and endpoint outcomes can be taken from the area of social sustainability. Many VSS include provisions in their standard catalogues that oblige certification holders to provide protective wear to workers when they perform tasks (such as the application of agrochemicals) that have been shown to have adverse health effects when improperly handled. Impact assessments interested in studying the effects of VSS on labour rights may well confirm that this protective wear has been provided to workers. Yet, it is another question whether workers actually use it, which, according to a recent study, is often not the case even when such protective equipment exists (Grabs 2020). Clearly, protective wear that is provided by certification holders presents a crucial step towards improving labour rights (intermediate outcomes). However, if workers do not use it in practice, the provision of protective wear has no real effect on increasing a workplace`s health and safety conditions (endpoint outcomes).

Form these examples, it becomes clear that the distinction between intermediate and endpoint variables matters conceptually (Oya el al 2018). Research that studies the sustainability effects of VSS through the lens of intermediate outcome variables is important because it helps us to understand the extent to which certified value chain actors implement the sustainability practices that VSS prescribe in their standard catalogues. However, only endpoint variables allow us to investigate whether VSS ultimately reach the sustainability goals they lay out in their theories of change. Endpoint variables thus present the more rigorous measures to study the sustainability effects and impacts of VSS on sustainable trade and production.

The TRANS SUSTAIN project identified 202 cases among the 176 articles in its literate database in which an article uses intermediate outcome variables to study the sustainability effects of VSS. Concerning these cases, the picture is clearly dominated by positive evaluations (41 per cent), followed by negative (35 per cent) and mixed evaluations (24 per cent). However, for cases (n=178) that evaluate the effects of VSS on sustainable production and trade based on endpoint variables, this picture changes dramatically. The percentage of positive evaluations decreases by almost 50 per cent, from 41 per cent of assessments to 22 per cent. Simultaneously, the percentage of negative evaluations increases from 35 per cent for intermediate outcomes to 45 per cent for endpoint variables. Mixed evaluations comprise a share of 33 per cent.

Of special concern are the results for cases in the area of economic sustainability. With their economic interventions, VSS aim to improve the economic situation of certified producers especially in developing countries. Intermediate outcomes variables to achieve economic sustainability goals include the payment of price premiums for standard compliant products, the provision of relevant technical and business trainings, or improved access to credit required for producers to make sustainable investments at their production sites. Interestingly, VSS turn out to be fairly effective in realizing these goals. The TRANS SUSTAIN literature database includes around 100 cases that evaluate the implementation of such intermediate economic outcome variables. Many of these cases (41 per cent) conclude with a positive evaluation indicating that VSS are largely able to realize these goals

in practice. In contrast to that, 36 per cent of the cases end with a negative evaluation while 23 per cent of the cases come to mixed results.

However, for cases that analyze whether these successes in the implementation of intermediate economic outcomes also turn into tangible improvements of living conditions of certified producers such as increased profits or increased wealth and well-being, the picture changes dramatically. For endpoint economic sustainability outcomes, the share of positive evaluations decreases significantly from 41 per cent to a share of only 16 per cent, while at the same time the share of negative evaluations rises from 36 per cent to 46 per cent percent. In other words, while cases that evaluate the capability of VSS to improve the economic conditions of certified producers based on intermediate outcome variables predominantly conclude with positive evaluations, cases that use endpoint variables overwhelmingly conclude with negative evaluations.

In the area of social sustainability, examples for intermediate outcomes include the provision of protective wear and first aids kits, the creation of grievance mechanisms to report misconduct, the building of workers' organizations and representative bodies, building schools, or the requirement to hire of workers based on written contracts with clearly defined (and delivered) wages. All of these intermediate outcomes present steps to improve endpoint livelihood outcomes such as increased workplace safety, improved health, or broader access to education. As becomes clear in Figure 10 most cases (49 per cent) that assessed the effects of VSS based on intermediate social outcome variables evaluate the capability of VSS to improve the social sustainability at certified production sites positively. However, this number decreases to 29 per cent in cases that evaluate the social impacts of VSS based on more rigorous social endpoint outcome variables. Here most cases (40 per cent) draw a negative conclusion about the capability of VSS to promote robust transitions to socially sustainable outcomes for producers.

Finally, a similar pattern emerges in the area of environmental sustainability. Although negative evaluations dominate the picture in cases that are based on intermediate and endpoint economic outcome variables, the rate of positive evaluations decreases by 10 points for cases that analyze endpoint environmental outcome variables, such as reduced CO2 emissions or increased biodiversity, to evaluate the performance of VSS to promote transitions to environmentally sustainable modes of production and trade.

Figure 10. Capabilities of VSS to increase intermediate and endpoint sustainability outcomes in available literature

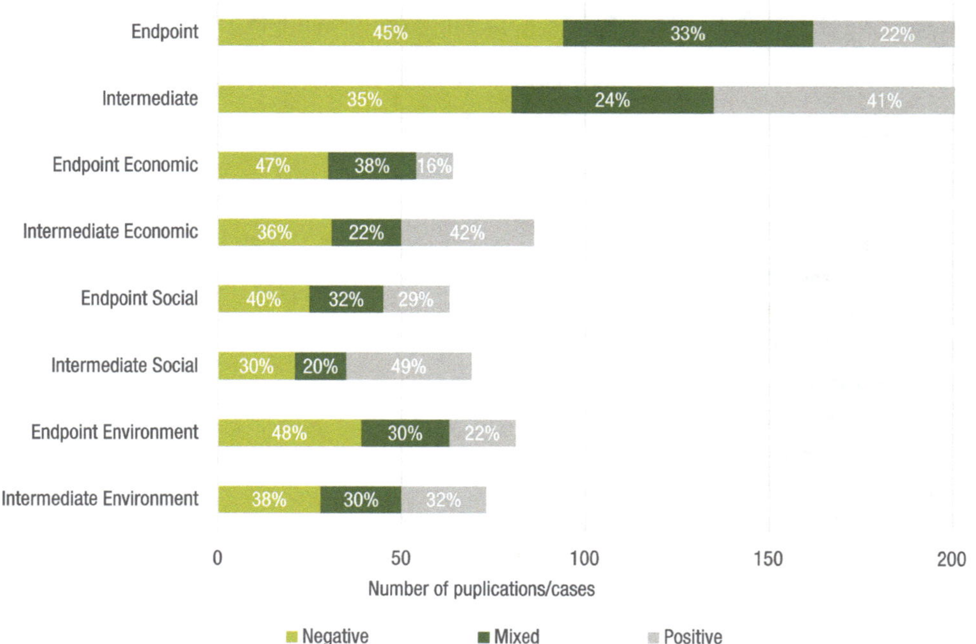

Concluding remarks and limitations

In sum, these results show that VSS are most successful at promoting behavioural changes towards more sustainable practices (intermediate outcomes). However, these changes do not translate into tangible and robust sustainability outcomes. We will further explain this gap in the next section. Overall, this study enhances the knowledge base for both scholars and decision-makers in politics, economics and civil society concerning the now widely-discussed question of whether the problem-solving capacity of VSS is significant enough to drive or bolster the urgently-needed sustainability transformations. Above, we outlined three major impacts of how the emergence of VSS could promote transitions towards better trade for sustainable development. These desired impacts were: (I) improving profit sharing between lead firms from developed and producers of primary goods in developed countries; (II) reconciling international trade with environmental sustainability goals; and (III) reconciling international trade with basic human and labour rights. Based on what is currently known about the sustainability effects of VSS on certified productions sites, we assess the problem-solving capacity of VSS to deliver on the above three goals is limited. Ground-level studies that have investigated the effects of VSS have found positive, mixed, and negative outcomes. However, all in all, negative evaluations prevail. In many cases, VSS adoption alone seems therefore not sufficient to promote substantial changes towards better trade for sustainable development.

At this point, the caveat needs to be stated that the evidence basis on which we can evaluate the effects and impacts of VSS on sustainable production and trade remains highly fragmented. The scholarly literature that has empirically assessed the sustainability effects of VSS is highly concentrated on the three sectors of forestry, (tropical) farm agriculture, and fisheries/aquaculture. The effects of VSS on sustainability outcomes at certified production sites in other important sectors, such as, for example, the manufacturing sector, have been very little researched so far. Moreover, the existing literature is highly concentrated on a few specific VSS, especially FSC and Fairtrade (see Figure 11). The most reliable results concern FSC and Fairtrade since they stand out as the two most studied individual VSS. With 48 per cent (FSC) and 50 per cent (Fairtrade) the results for these two VSS show a share of negative evaluations above the average of 42,6 per cent what again fits into the picture of the overall limited effectiveness of VSS promoting sustainable change.

Figure 11. **Distribution of positive, mixed and negative evaluations over individual VSS in the available literature**

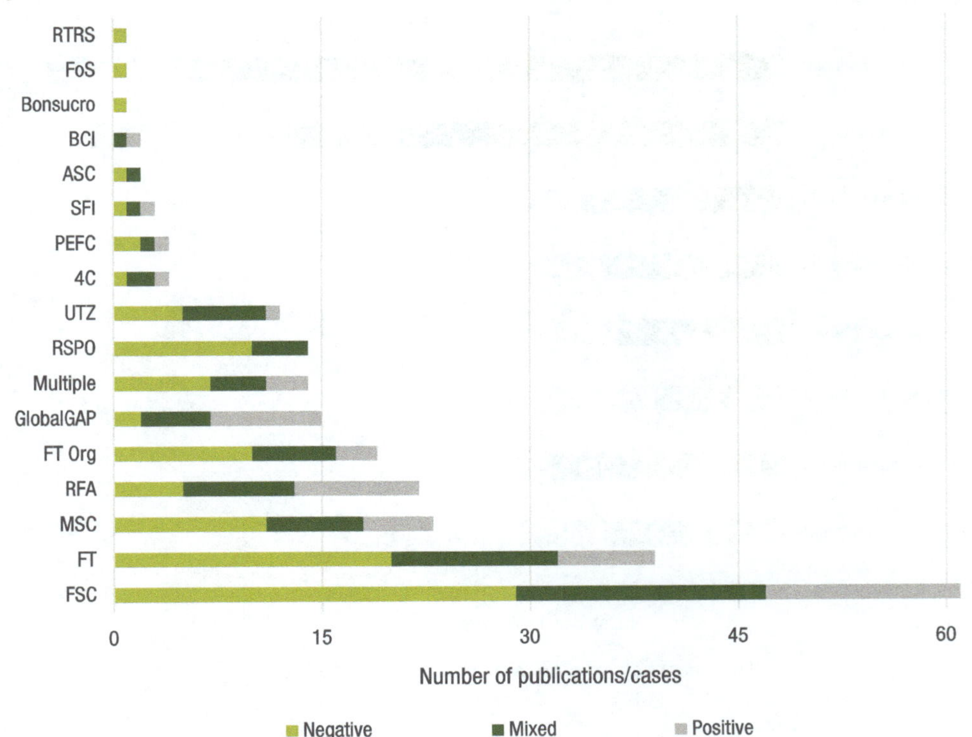

Figure 12 demonstrates the geographic distribution of studies in our literature base by country. On the level of individual countries, most cases address production sites in Kenya and Indonesia. On a regional level, Latin America has the highest number of cases. Together with North America, Latin America is also the region with largest geographic coverage. In term of cases, Latin America is followed by Africa and Asia. However, country coverage is lower in these regions than it is in Latin America. In Europe, coverage is fragmented between cases focusing the Scandinavian countries on the one hand, and Portugal, Spain and Turkey on the other. In absolute terms, only two countries, Kenya and Indonesia, show more than 10 case studies wherein the effects of VSS on sustainable production and trade have been analyzed. For many other countries, the TRANS SUSTAIN database either found no studies whatsoever that suited our (rather generous) parameters, or only very few (between 5 and 10). In other words, we still need to increase the evidence base significantly before we will be able to draw any definite conclusions about the effects and impacts of VSS on improving sustainable production and trade.

Figure 12. Overview about the countries of certified production sites studied by the available literature

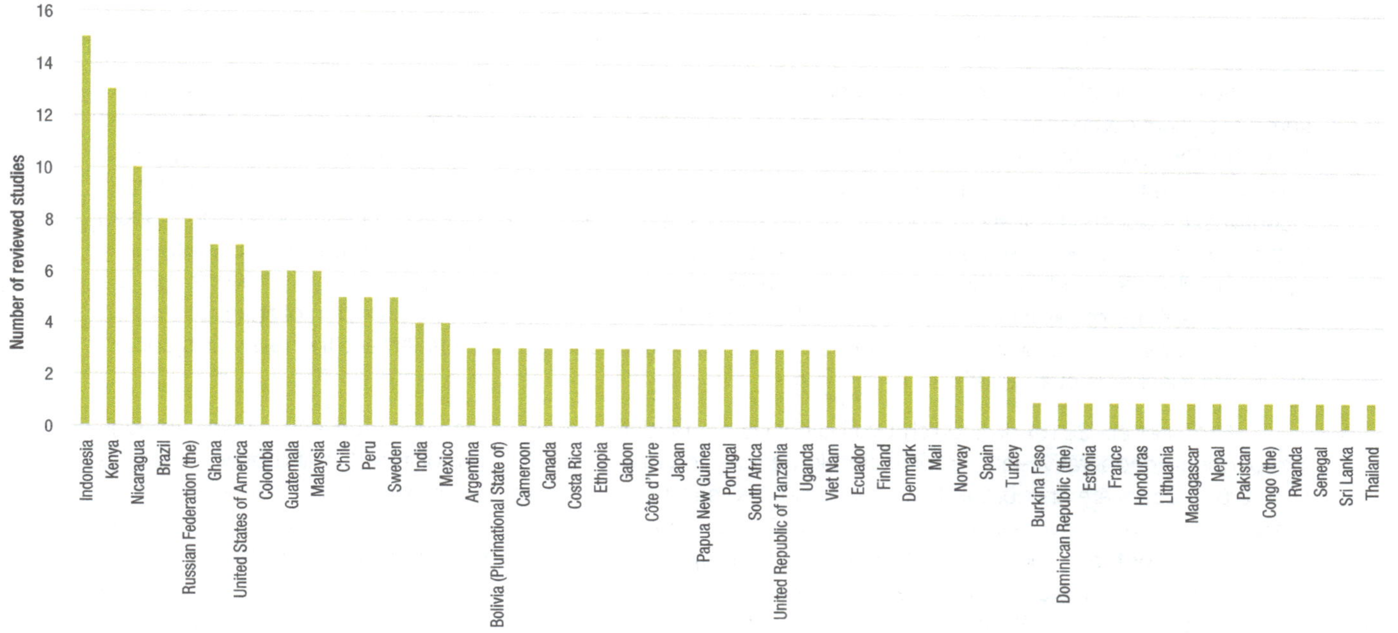

4.4 CHALLENGES OF VSS EFFECTIVENESS IN DEVELOPING COUNTRIES

Most studies that assess the impacts of VSS on economic, environmental or social sustainability outcomes focus on certified production sites in developing country contexts in Latin America, Africa and Asia. According to the results we presented in the previous sections of this report, the impacts that VSS have on sustainable production and trade in these regions remains limited. So why is this the case? Why doesn't VSS certification, in many cases, ultimately improve the economic situation of certified producers? Why do VSS so often fail to significantly reduce the ecological footprint and basic social conditions at certified production sites? Finally, what are the major challenges that VSS must overcome so that meaningful and tangible changes towards sustainable production and outcomes follow adoption? In the following section we develop an answer to this question by drawing on crucial insights from the policy implementation literature.

Ensuring implementation

For VSS to improve the sustainability of certified production and trade beyond the status quo, VSS need to specify strict sustainability standards. Second, VSS must ensure that after standard adoption, certified producers successfully implement and maintain these standards. The policy implementation literature identifies two pathways by which challenging policies can be effectively implemented on the ground: top-down or bottom-up. The top-down perspective argues for the importance of a hierarchical chain of command and the definition of clear policy objectives, which allows for an optimal diffusion of policymakers' intents on the ground. The bottom-up perspective, in contrast, foregrounds the important role played by producers, who develop new (or reshape existing) policies to solve everyday problems (Sabatier 1986). Both perspectives broadly agree that successful implementation of policies hinges on two central factors (Hill and Hupe 2014; Sabatier 1986): first, targeted actors need clear incentives for compliance, which may include credible threats of sanctions (in the case of non-compliance), and/or the delivery of promised benefits that result from compliance. Second, the existence of institutional resources and capacity for both implementation and enforcement is paramount for on-the-ground success (Schneider und Ingram 1990).

Implementation and effectiveness in VSS governance systems

While the implementation literature has focused mostly on state-level and multi-level public policies, the same analytical components and conditions for success hold true for the implementation of private regulations through VSS. Given their voluntary status, the adoption of such standards only makes sense if they provide a positive business case for implementing actors (Vogel 2008). In the absence of such positive economic incentives, producers are likely to drop out. There is also a need for effective linkage of incentives to performance, in the absence of which we are unlikely to observe behavioural change. In addition, given that VSS frequently target small-scale producers in developing countries, there is significant need for capacity-building on the ground. Examples of this include repeated small-group training sessions and/or the provision of financial support for upfront investments, which helps to ensure that producers successfully implement the relevant standard provisions (Raynolds et al. 2004).

Grabs et al. (2016) distinguish two pathways of standard adoption: the supply-driven pathway (through independent, cooperative-led, or institution-led efforts to achieve certification) or the demand-driven pathway (where producers are encouraged to achieve certified status by exporters, final processors, or retailers). In both scenarios, producers whose practices already closely align with the requirements demanded by certifiers are more likely to opt into certification. The closer existing practices are to complying with certification, the lower the costs that producers or downstream value chain actors must invest to qualify for certification. As Bitzer et al. (2008) have argued, VSS adoption usually first takes root in niche markets by primarily reaching out to the so-called "low-hanging fruits", who comprise a relatively small group of producers that are already producing in relatively sustainable ways. Yet, due to this selection effect, the impacts of VSS on sustainable production and trade are limited to these niche markets, since in these cases standards do little more than certifying pre-existing behaviour.

VSS implementation gaps in developing country contexts

The "low-hanging fruit" problem is particularly virulent in the context of developing countries. It is the smallest producers in particular who often lack the financial means to adapt their production practices to VSS requirements, leaving them excluded from access to standard compliant markets and their associated price premiums. The adaptation costs that these small producers must incur to comply with VSS production requirements rise considerably as compared to the "low-hanging fruit". Such costs include one-off investments in training, cleaner production infrastructure, compliance with health and safety requirements, as well as ongoing costs related to improving the living standards of workers and sacrificing short-term productivity for environmentally beneficial practices.

The crucial problem is the highly unequal profit sharing between lead firms in developed countries and producers in developing countries that heavily reduces the certification potentiality to economically empower producers in developing countries to adopt and maintain improved sustainability practices. For such a development to materialize, both the price premiums for standard compliant products and the resources provided by downstream value chain actors to support producers would need to increase exponentially. Yet, recent studies suggest that the financial resources provided to producers for VSS implementation have not increased at the required rate (Dietz and Grabs 2021). The consumer-end premiums still remain largely restricted to niche markets in western countries. Further, especially in VSS front-runner sectors (such as coffee), we currently observe a trend in which leading companies abandon third-party certification systems in favour of developing their own in-house sustainability programs.

The resources generated through certification systems to facilitate the implementation of sustainable practices thus appear to stagnate — or even, in some cases, decline. As a result, the expansion of sustainability certifications to poorer producers in developing contexts increases the per-unit resources required to deliver comprehensive sustainability transformations (Curve A), while the provision of these required resources is simultaneously decreasing (Curve B). VSS therefore face a situation in which producers in developing contexts increasingly lack the resources (area in grey) to effectively implement more sustainable production practices.

Figure 13. The resource gap of VSS implementation in developing countries (adapted from Dietz and Grabs 2021)

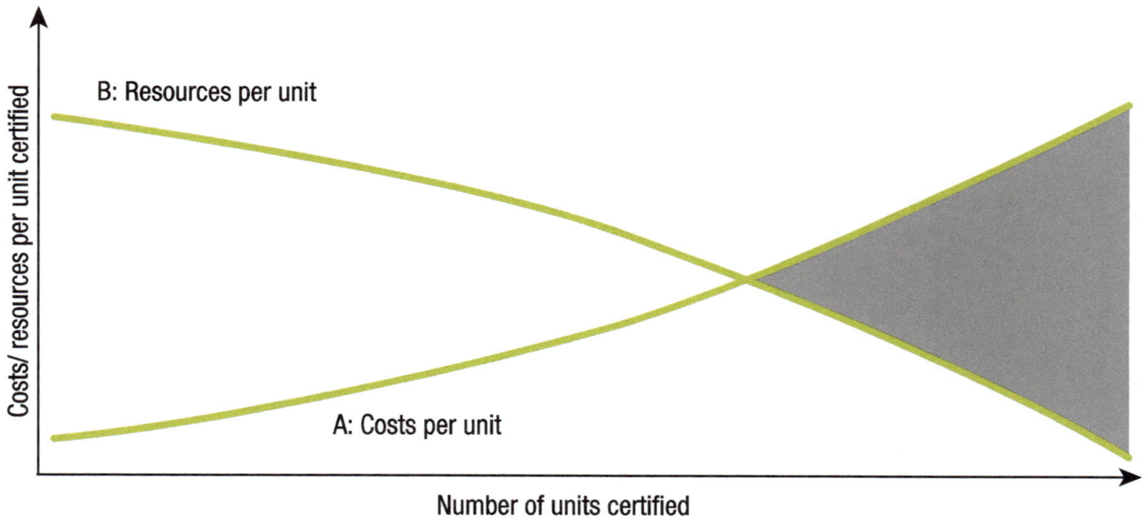

The growing gap between the financial resources generated through VSS systems and the resources needed to enable producers in developing countries to implement meaningful sustainability standards, leads to three major problems. First, especially disadvantaged producers who are at greatest need of assistance if they are to improve their production practices are systematically crowded out from existing certification schemes. Second, especially when VSS allow for large group certification with less strict auditing requirements, the occurrence of compliance gaps rises dramatically, simply because producers lack the resources and capacity to implement meaningful sustainability standards. Third, VSS that compete for market shares face huge challenges to expand certification beyond those producers who already operate largely in compliance with certification requirements, while producers who generally lack the resources to shift towards more sustainable modes of production are left behind. Under such conditions, it is often the VSS themselves that adapt to new circumstances by lowering the stringency of their standards and certification processes in order to include ever more producers in their system. In sum, the greatest challenge VSS currently face in developing countries to catalyze the implementation of more sustainable practices is to generate more financial resources per certified unit. This would empower poorer and less sustainable producers to manage the necessary sustainability transformations.

To be sure, there are further challenges to VSS effectiveness in developing country contexts. For example, normative standards developed in developed countries may not translate easily to local cultures in developing countries, where their implementation most often takes place (Hatanaka 2010). Further, organizational drawbacks, lack of transparency, the capture of certified products' added retail value by other value chain actors, and corruption that may undermine public policies can all have negative bearings on the administration and outcomes of private certification schemes. Concretely, price premiums may be withheld from smallholder producers by managing entities, living wages may not be provided, or conventional products may be falsely declared as standard compliant. However, such kinds of problems are ultimately of a practical nature and could be solved if VSS successfully address this fundamental challenge: certification must generate more resources for producers if they are to achieve their aim of enabling transformative sustainability changes in developing country contexts.

5. CONCLUSION AND POLICY RECOMMENDATIONS

International trade has grown significantly over the last decades. Besides an increase in trade we also witnessed a change in the nature of trade through the emergence of global value chains. International trade is now predominantly conducted through global value chains which link producers in developing countries to consumers around the globe. Addressing social and environmental issues in global value chains has also received increased attention with the emergence of the concept of sustainable development and its inclusion in the 2030 Global Agenda and Sustainable Development Goals. The link in GVCs between consumers and producers and the increasing attention to sustainable development offers an opportunity for VSS to contribute significantly to sustainable development. This report focused on the role VSS can play. The potential of VSS to make trade more sustainable relies on two crucial components: first that they generate an impact on the ground and second that they are widely used. We discussed these two components in-depth and showed the progress made so far and the challenges which remain.

Concerning impact, we showed that VSS define complex sets of standards to ensure the production and trade of standards-compliant products. These standards contain economic, environmental and social regulations. In addition, VSS may include standards that do not focus on the regulatory control but the empowerment of certified producers. Such standards require greater commitments and more collaboration by downstream value chain actors.

We have identified three major impacts of how VSS may improve trade relations, given the appropriate conditions and support, thereby fostering sustainable development: (I) The improvement of profit and power-sharing between lead firms from developed countries and producers of primary goods in developing countries (*economic sustainability*) (II) the reconciliation of international trade with environmental sustainability and (III) and the reconciliation of international trade with basic human and labour rights (social sustainability). From a policy perspective, one pivotal issue is to assess the extent to which VSS indeed reach these goals especially in the context of developing countries.

Our review shows that the pertinent literature that has investigated the impacts of VSS on the ground reaches different conclusions. While some evaluate the effects of VSS on sustainable trade positively, many articles question the capability of VSS to promote substantial changes towards more sustainable modes of production and trade. While VSS are most successful at promoting behavioural changes towards more sustainable practices (intermediate outcomes) these changes do not necessarily translate into tangible and robust sustainability outcomes (endpoint outcomes). Given these results, which especially refer to the context of developing countries, it is important to note that despite the rise of a now extensive body of literature that has assessed the impacts of VSS on the ground, the evidence is still too limited to draw any firm conclusions.

Transitions towards more sustainable trade require substantial investments into sustainable GVCs. The crucial problem is that the implementation of current VSS systems is not profitable enough for producers in developing countries to economically empower them to adopt and maintain improved sustainability practices. VSS provide one important potential to promote sustainability, but the resources are still too limited to enable profound changes towards sustainable trade. Critically, existing VSS systems often fail to reach producers and the environment in developing countries that need the most support to transition towards more sustainable modes of production.

Concerning uptake, we showed that there is significant variation in the use of VSS across countries and commodities and identified four barriers related to the uptake of VSS:

- A first barrier is constituted by the costs involved in receiving certification and the inability of producers in specific countries to obtain certification.

- A second barrier relates to a lack of incentives to gain certification.

- A third barrier results from what we called a governance gap which refers to the fact that producers in many developing countries operate in a regulatory context which is not aligned with the regulatory approach of VSS.

- A final barrier refers to political dynamics and possible opposition towards VSS which are either perceived as or are de facto mainly a Western version of market-based governance for sustainability which is not shared by everyone.

5.1 POLICY RECOMMENDATIONS

Addressing the challenges identified in this report to enhance VSS effectiveness can be addressed via different policy recommendations. We consider four key mechanisms for more structural change and transformation.

First: Leveraging the support by donors and multilateral organizations

Several actors could take action to address the barriers identified above. International organizations and donor agencies can help address some barriers, especially in developing countries, and have also done so. International multilateral organizations and donor agencies have directly and indirectly encouraged the adoption of VSS as a means of achieving the interlocking objectives of the inclusion of developing economies into global trade through a transparent set of standards, which, in turn, embody the principles of sustainability. Multilateral organizations and donors can continue their engagement with VSS in order to overcome some of the barriers identified above. Donors and multilateral organizations have specifically focused their attention on certain challenges with which VSS are confronted as a tool for sustainable development.

There are many examples of projects of national and international multilateral donors to support the use of VSS. They provide financial and technical support to various VSS. Most European technical cooperation bodies are involved in supporting VSS. For instance, UNCTAD has developed a VSS Assessment Toolkit that facilitates a reality-check conducted in the field. It aims to identify challenges and perceptions behind VSS adoption and explore policy options to address them.[13] In addition, ITC has developed the T4SD Global Database to analyze very diverse standards initiatives. ITC collects, reviews and categorizes the requirements and processes of standards information. The database is built upon some 1,000 data points, developed with technical partners and over 200 standard organizations. It is revised annually to accommodate more sectors and requirements. Moreover, UNFSS, a collaboration between five United Nations agencies (FAO, ITC, UNCTAD, UN Environment, and UNIDO) serves as a neutral and credible platform to maximize the potential of VSS as a means to achieve the SDGs through facilitating emerging economies access to lucrative markets, stimulating well-informed dialogue among key stakeholders at the national and international level, and building capacities for producers and SMEs, to enhance opportunities in international trade.

While details of donor support are easily accessible on the websites of these organizations, there are very few studies that document the different modalities of donor-VSS involvement and interaction; and how the resulting partnership dynamics affect sustainable development efforts (Lambin 2014). Humphrey (2008) provides a case study of analyzing the role played by DIFID and USAID in the implementation of the GlobalGAP standard in the Kenyan horticulture sector and shows that donor involvement was an important element for VSS to take root in Kenyan horticulture. Hoang et al (2015) analyze the benefits (higher prices and access to markets) and challenges (increased complexity of production) of FSC certification for Vietnamese small household groups. Their study shows that in Viet Nam there was a significant standards compliance gap (see above) between the pre-certification state of forests and the state necessary to obtain certification (see also Putzel, 2012). In order to close this gap Hoang et al. show that there was/is a heavy dependency on donors for financial and technical

---

[13] For more info see https://vssapproach.unctad.org/toolkit/ and https://unctad.org/project/fostering-green-exports-through-voluntary-sustainability-standards-developing-countries

support. A similar result was presented by Duchelle et al. (2014) who analyzed certification in the tri-national border region of Bolivia, Brazil, and Peru. These paper shows that partnerships with cooperatives, donors, government and nongovernmental organizations are essential to maximize conservation and development objectives from VSS.

Second: Integrating VSS in Public Policy

A first structural approach would be to more systematically integrate VSS in public policy instruments and make them part of hybrid policy-arrangements to address sustainability issues. This is already occurring and an increasing body of literature is focusing on the integration of VSS in public policies (Renckens, 2020) and so-called public-private interactions. This literature highlights that VSS operate in different regulatory environments that can range from being fully supportive to being conflictual, with various in-between types of interactions. As Bell and Hindmoor (2012) argue, public-private relations were initially conceived as a zero-sum game, in which either the private entity or the state takes the regulatory lead at the other's expense. However, this perspective has been challenged, as public-private interactions have appeared more diversified. Lambin et al. (2014) characterize public-private interactions as being either complementary, substitutive, or antagonistic. Complementarity involves states creating an enabling regulatory environment for VSS to operate in, and VSS reinforcing public regulations or filling in a policy gap; substitution refers to governments absorbing existing VSS in public policies or laws thus transforming private rules into public ones; and antagonism occurs when public and private rules prescribe conflicting practices.

Marques and Eberlein (2020) go further and distinguish five types of public-private interactions. First, VSS can act as *substitutes* to public rules for matters which States are unable or unwilling to regulate and thus fulfil a regulatory gap, similarly to Lambin et al.'s (2014) complementarity. Second, States can *adopt and support* private rules in different ways, including acting as clients by adopting certification for state-led production operations; providing administrative or financial support to enable domestic firms to comply with VSS; offering political endorsement to VSS; or enacting policies that recognise VSS as proof of compliance with public requirements. Third, states can build on existing VSS and *repurpose* them to better fit public objectives. Fourth, when VSS are perceived as a threat to state sovereignty or are inconsistent with public strategic priorities, states can *reject* private rules and obstruct their operations. Fifth, when they have the capacity to do so, states can *replace* VSS with public rules. The fourth and the fifth type of interaction will negatively affect the adoption of VSS, but the first three will positively affect the adoption of VSS.

Overall, the literature has highlighted the diversity of potential interactions between public and private rules and has assumed that state's support for VSS is a driver for their adoption. Some concrete examples further illustrate this integration of VSS in public policy:

- First, VSS are becoming a key component of policies on sustainable public procurement. Sustainable public procurement, i.e. the use of government spending to pursue sustainable development, is gaining ground both in developed as well as developing countries. VSS play an important role in the operationalisation of sustainable public procurement and many governments use VSS as an indication that the products they buy are made more sustainable (D'Hollander & Marx, 2014).

- Second, an increasing number of free trade agreements, especially those involving the European Union as a party, promote cooperation and information sharing about VSS (UNFSS, 2020). Some trade and economic partnership agreements, such as the recently signed between EFTA countries (Norway, Iceland, Liechtenstein and Switzerland) and Indonesia, even provide for applying lower tariffs for certified products with regard to specific commodities such as palm oil.

- Third, an increasing number of regulations are integrating VSS as part of due diligence requirements to regulate global value chains. Examples include the European Union Timber Regulation, the Republic of Korea Act on the Sustainable Use of Timbers and different regulatory initiatives which aim to implement some form of mandatory human rights due diligence.

- Fourth, several developing countries use and support VSS in the context of the export promotion. The 4th UNFSS flagship (2020) details several examples of the use of VSS to promote export.

These examples and the literature on public-private interactions illustrate the important role governments can play in influencing the adoption and use of VSS. Expanding the uptake of VSS could enhance their overall impact. Indeed, in various ways VSS can complement other policy approaches and by further integrating VSS in public policies they might be scaled up and achieve a more significant impact.

Third: Further harness the market-based potential of VSS by providing more transparency to consumers

The cumulative impact of the proliferation of VSS on increasing sustainability as a whole is currently not possible to measure precisely. This has a multitude of causes. First, different certifications define sustainability in radically different ways. There remains no standardized, authoritative definition of what sustainable production would look like, so there is no objective benchmark against which to measure VSS environmental and social performance. Even the SDGs, arguably the most comprehensive framework for understanding sustainability challenges and potential solutions, provide guiding principles rather than prescriptive roadmaps, with a degree of margin of interpretation of how to implement them in any particular landscape or community. Second, the majority of the data collected on VSS utilization belongs to the VSS themselves and are rarely made public.

The need for further work on the impact of sustainability goals combined with a lack of transparency about VSS impacts on the ground presents a serious governance barrier for VSS. Economic actors along GVCs adopt and implement VSS in order to get access to standard complaint markets or to protect their brand reputations. VSS adoption signals sustainable behaviour. Ethical consumers may reward sustainably produced products with price premiums. However, without clearly defined sustainability measures and a lack of transparency about the impacts of VSS on the ground, consumers lack sufficient information to reliably distinguish effective from ineffective VSS. Under such conditions, effective VSS keep facing difficulties to prevail against less strict alternatives. In order to survive in a competitive standards market, stricter VSS may instead be forced to adopt their standards catalogues to their weaker competitors.

One possibility for policy-makers to interfere with this logic of a "race to the bottom" could be to intensify the multi-stakeholder dialogues with private governance actors in order to nudge VSS to adopt a common regulatory framework with measurable sustainable targets and clearly defined transparency rules that apply to all schemes. In doing so, policy makers could help create an equal playing field for VSS that could lift up the overall sustainability performance of these governance schemes. This 'harmonization' can be pursued through at least two mechanisms:

- One is for governments and maybe even international organizations to set up recognition systems which distinguish credible from non-credible standards. This is akin to the idea of certifying the certifiers. Such a mechanism would identify those VSS which contribute more significantly to sustainable development based on a set of criteria.

- The second mechanism is that governments or international organizations support and promote mutual recognition between VSS. Mutual recognition entails that VSS recognize each other as being equivalent in terms of standards and conformity assessment. The current level of mutual recognition between VSS is very low (Marx & Wouters, 2015). Promoting mutual recognition might foster the development of common regulatory frameworks between VSS.

Fourth: Strengthening Empowerment

VSS should strengthen the empowerment potential of their systems to create stronger incentives for producers and other actors to use and adopt VSS. VSS schemes need to address power imbalances that marginalize producers and to place fairness at the heart of economic relations to transform trade. Sharing power with and strengthening smallholders create higher incentives for producers and other actors to use and adopt

VSS. Addressing power imbalances is not only through price premium and value sharing; it exceeds that to redesigning the ways decisions are made to include actors from the back-end of the value chain. This can be achieved by giving producers a stronger voice in high levels of leadership and involving their representation on the standard setting committee.

REFERENCES

Abbott K and Snidal D (2009). The Governance Triangle: Regulatory Standards Institutions and the Shadow of the State. In Whose Benefit? Explaining Regulatory Change in Global Politics. *The Politics of Global Regulation*. Walter Mattli & Ngaire Woods, eds: 44-88.

Aguilar F and Vlosky R (2007). Consumer willingness to pay price premiums for environmentally certified wood products in the US. *Forest Policy and Economics*. 9: 1100-1112.

Ansell C and Vogel D (2006). Whats the Beef? The Contested Governance of European Food Safety. MIT Press working paper.

Ascoly N and Zeldenrust I (2003). Considering Complaint Mechanisms. An important tool for code monitoring and verification. Amsterdam: SOMO.

Auld G (2014). Constructing Private Governance: The Rise and Evolution of Forest, Coffee, and Fisheries Certification. Yale University Press.

Auld G and Renckens S (2021). Private sustainability governance, the Global South and COVID-19: Are changes to audit policies in light of the pandemic exacerbating existing inequalities? *World Development. 139.*

Auld G, Renckens S and Cashore B (2014). Transnational private governance between the logics of empowerment and control. *Regulation and Governance. 9:* 108-124.

Barenberg M (2008). Toward a Democratic Model of Transnational Labour Monitoring? In: Bercusson, B and Estlund C (eds.) *Regulating Labour in the Wake of Globalisation*. Hart Publishers. 37-65.

Bartley T (2003). Certifying forests and factories: States, social movements, and the rise of private regulation in the apparel and forest products fields. *Politics and Society*.31 (3): 433-464.

Bartley T (2007). Institutional Emergence in an Era of Globalization: The Rise of Transnational Private Regulation of Labor and Environmental Conditions. *American Journal of Sociology*. 113(2):297-351.

Bartley T (2010). Transnational Private Regulation in Practice: The Limits of Forest and Labor Standards Certification in Indonesia. *Business and Politics.* 12(3): 1-34.

Bartley T (2011). Certification as a mode of social regulation. In Levi-Faur D (ed.) Handbook on the Politics of Regulation. Cheltenham: Edward Elgar:441– 452.

Bartley T (2014). Transnational governance and the re-centered state: sustainability or legality? *Regulation and Governance*. 8:93-109.

Bartley T (2018). Rules without Rights. Land, Labor and Private Authority in the Global Economy. Oxford: Oxford University Press.

Basso V M, Jacovine L A G, Alves R R, Valverde S R, da Silva F L, Brianezi D (2011). Evaluation of the influence of forest certification in compliance with environmental legislation in forest plantations. *Revista Arvore*, 35(4):835-844.

Basso V, Jacovine L A G, Alves R R and Nardelli A (2012). Contribution of forest certification in the attendance to the environmental and social legislation in Minas Gerais State. *Revista Arvore.* 36(4):747-757.

Bell S and Hindmoor A (2012). Governance Without Government? The Case of the Forest Stewardship Council. *Public Administration*. 90(1)144–159.

Bennet E A (2018). Voluntary Sustainability Standards: A Squandered Opportunity to Improve Workers Wages. *Sustainable Development*. 26(1):65-82.

Bennett E A (2017). Who Governs Socially-Oriented Voluntary Sustainability Standards? Not the Producers of Certified Products. *World Development*. 91:53-69.

Biermann F, Norichika K, and Rakhyun E K (2017) Global Governance by Goal Setting: The novel approach of the UN Sustainable Development Goals. *Current Opinion in Environmental Sustainability*. 26-31.

Bissinger K, Brandi C, Cabrera de Leicht S, Fiorini M, Schleifer P, Fernandez de Cordova S, and Elamin N (2020). Linking Voluntary Standards to Sustainable Development Goals. International Trade Centre, Geneva, Switzerland.

Blackman A and Rivera J (2011). Producer-level benefits of sustainability certification. *Conservation Biology*.25(6):1176–1185. DOI: 10.1111/j.1523-1739.2011.01774.x.

Bloomfield M (2020). South-South trade and sustainable development: the case of Ceylon tea.*Ecological Economics*. 167.

Blumroeder J S, Burova N, Winter S, Goroncy, A, Hobsonm P R and Shegolev A (2019). Ecological effects of clearcutting practices in a boreal forest (Arkhangelsk Region, Russian Federation) both with and without FSC certification. *Ecological Indicators*: 106. DOI: 10.1016/j.ecolind.2019.105461.

Bouslah K, MZali B, Turcotte M F and Kooli M (2010). The Impact of Forest Certification on Firm Financial Performance in Canada and the U.S. *Journal of Business Ethics*. 96 (4),551–572. DOI: 10.1007/s10551-010-0482-5.

Bradford A (2020). The Brussels Effect. How the European Union Rules the World. Oxford: Oxford University Press.

Bright C, Marx A, Pineau N and J Wouters (2020). Towards a corporate duty for lead companies to respect human rights in their global value chains? *Business and Politics*. 22(4):667-697.

Burivalova Z, Hua F, Koh L P, Garcia C and Putz F (2017). A Critical Comparison of Conventional, Certified, and Community Management of Tropical Forests for Timber in Terms of Environmental, Economic, and Social Variables. *CONSERVATION LETTERS*. 10(1):4–14. DOI: 10.1111/conl.12244.

Büthe T (2010). Private Regulation in the Global Economy: A (P)Review. *Business Politics*. 12(3):1–38. DOI: 10.2202/1469-3569.1328.

Carlson A and Palmer C (2016). A qualitative meta-synthesis of the benefits of eco-labeling in developing countries. *Ecological Economics*.127:129–145. DOI: 10.1016/j.ecolecon.2016.03.020.

Carter D P, Scott T A, and Mahallati N (2018). Balancing barriers to entry and administrative burden in voluntary regulation. Perspectives on Public Management and Governance, 1(3), 207–221.

Cashore B, Auld G and Newsom D (2004). Governing Through Markets: Forest Certification and the Emergence of Non-State Authority. New Haven: Yale University Press.

Castaneda-Navarrete J, Hauge J and López-Gómez C (2020). COVID-19s impacts on global value chains, as seen in the apparel industry. *Development Policy Review*. 10.1111/dpr.12539.

Cattau M E, Marlier M E and DeFries R (2016). Effectiveness of Roundtable on Sustainable Palm Oil (RSPO) for reducing fires on oil palm concessions in Indonesia from 2012 to 2015. *Environmental Research Letters*. 11(10). DOI: 10.1088/1748-9326/11/10/105007.

Collins B, Evans A and Hung M (2017). The New Regulators? Assessing the Landscape of Multi-Stakeholder Initiatives.. MSI Integrity and Kenan Institute for Ethics, Duke University.

Cramer C, Johnston D, Mueller B, Oya C, Sender J (2017). Fairtrade and Labour Markets in Ethiopia and Uganda. *Journal of Development Studies*.53(6):841–856. DOI: 10.1080/00220388.2016.1208175.

Cuyvers L and T De Meyer (2012). Market-driven promotion of international labour standards in Southeast Asia: the corporatization of social justice, Marx A, Maertens M Swinnen J and Wouters J (eds.). *Global Governance and Private Standards*. Interdisciplinary Perspectives. Cheltenham: Edward Elgar. 114-149.

DeFries R S, Fanzo J, Mondal P, Remans R, Wood S A (2017). Is voluntary certification of tropical agricultural commodities achieving sustainability goals for small-scale producers? A review of the evidence. *Environmental Research Letters* 12(3): 33001. DOI: 10.1088/1748-9326/aa625e.

D'Hollander D and Marx A (2014). Strengthening Private Certification Systems through Public Regulation: The Case Of Sustainable Public Procurement: *Sustainability Accounting, Management and Policy Journal*. 5(1): 2-22.

Dietz T, Auffenberg J, Estrella C A, Grabs J, Kilian B (2018). The Voluntary Coffee Standard Index (VOCSI). Developing a Composite Index to Assess and Compare the Strength of Mainstream Voluntary Sustainability Standards in the Global Coffee Industry. *Ecological Economics*. 150:72–87. DOI: 10.1016/j. ecolecon.2018.03.026.

Dietz T, Estrella C A, Grabs J, Kilian B (2020). How Effective is Multiple Certification in Improving the Economic Conditions of Smallholder Farmers? Evidence from an Impact Evaluation in Colombias Coffee Belt. *The Journal of Development Studies*. 56(6):1141–1160. DOI: 10.1080/00220388.2019.1632433.

Dietz T, Grabs J (2021). Additionality and Implementation Gaps in Voluntary Sustainability Standards. *New Political Economy*.1–22. DOI: 10.1080/13563467.2021.1881473.

Dingwerth K (2007). The New Transnationalism: transnational governance and democratic legitimacy Basingstoke: Palgrave Macmillan.

Duchelle AE, Kainer KA, Wadt LHO (2014). Is Certification Associated with Better Forest Management and Socioeconomic Benefits? A Comparative Analysis of Three Certification Schemes Applied to Brazil Nuts in Western Amazonia.*Society and Natural Resources.*27(2):121-139.

Dupuy L and Agarwal M (2014). International trade and sustainable development. In: Atkinson G, Dietz S, Neumayer E and Agarwala M (ed.). *Handbook of Sustainable Development*, Edward Elgar Publishing. 399-417.

Elamin N and Fernandez de Cordoba S (2020). The Trade Impact of Voluntary Sustainability Standards: A review of empirical evidence. Research Paper No 50. UNCTAD.

Esbenshade J (2004). Monitoring Sweatshops: Workers, consumers and the global apparel industry. Philadelphia

ESCAP and UNCTAD (2019). *ASIA-PACIFIC TRADE AND INVESTMENT REPORT 2019. Navigating Non-tariff Measures towards Sustainable Development*. (United Nations publication Sales No. E.19.II.F.14).

Espinoza O and Dockry M J (2014). Forest Certification in Bolivia: A Status Report and Analysis of Stakeholder Perspectives. *Forest Products Journal* 64(3–4):80–89.

Fayet L and Vermeulen W (2014). Supporting Smallholders to Access Sustainable Supply Chains: Lessons from the Indian Cotton Supply Chain. *Sustainable Development* 22(5): 289-310.

Fayet L and Vermeulen W (2014). Supporting Smallholders to Access Sustainable Supply Chains: Lessons from the Indian Cotton Supply Chain. *Sustainable Development* 22(5):289–310. DOI: 10.1002/sd.1540.

Fiankor D D D, Martínez-Zarzoso I and Brümmer B (2019). Exports and governance: the role of private voluntary agrifood standards. *Agricultural Economics*. 50(3): 341-352 https://doi.org/10.1111/agec.12488.

Fiorini M, Hoekman B, Jansen M, Schleifer P, Solleder O, Taimasova R and Wozniak J (2018). Institutional design of voluntary sustainability standards systems: Evidence from a new database. *Development Policy Review*. 37(S2): O193-O212.

Fortunato P (2020). How COVID-19 is changing global value chains. Retrieved from https://unctad.org/news/how-covid-19-changing-global-value-chains.

Froese R and Proelss A (2012). Evaluation and legal assessment of certified seafood. *Marine Policy* 36(6): 1284–1289. DOI: 10.1016/j.marpol.2012.03.017.

Garcia-Johnson R (2000). Exporting Environmentalism. US Multinational Chemical Corporations in Brazil and Mexico. MIT Press.

Garrett R D, Carlson K M, Rueda X and Noojipady P (2016). Assessing the potential additionality of certification by the Round table on Responsible Soybeans and the Roundtable on Sustainable Palm Oil. *Environmental Research Letters.* 11 (4). DOI: 10.1088/1748-9326/11/4/045003.

Garrett R D, Levy S, Gollnow F, Hodel L and Rueda X (2021). Have food supply chain policies improved forest conservation and rural livelihoods? A systematic review. Environmental Research Letter. 16(3) 033002. DOI: 10.1088/1748-9326/abe0ed.

Gereffi G and Fernandez-Stark K (2011). Global Value Chain Analysis: A Primer. Durham: Center on Globalization, Governance and Competitiveness.

Gereffi G and Lee J (2014). Economic and social upgrading in global value chains and industrial clusters: Why governance matters. *Journal of Business Ethics.* 133:25-38.

Gereffi G (2001) The NGO–Industrial Complex. *Foreign Policy.*125:56–65.

Gereffi G and Humphrey J and Sturgeon T (2005). The Governance of Global Value Chain. *Review of international political economy.* 12:78–104. 10.1080/09692290500049805.

Grabs J (2020) Selling Sustainability Short? The private governance of labour and the environment in the coffee sector? Cambridge: Cambridge University Press.

Grabs J, Kilian B, Hernandez D C and Dietz T (2016). Understanding Coffee Certification Dynamics: A Spatial Analysis of Voluntary Sustainability Standard Proliferation. *International Food and Agribusiness Management Review.* 19 (3):1-26.

Graffham A, Karehu E and MacGregor J (2007). Impact of EurepGAP on small-scale vegetable growers in Kenya. Fresh Insights.

Hatanaka M (2010). Governing sustainability: examining audits and compliance in a third-party-certified organic shrimp farming project in rural Indonesia. *Local Environment.* 15 (3):233–244. DOI: 10.1080/13549830903575588.

Henson S and Jaffee S (2008). Understanding developing country strategic responses to the enhancement of food safety standards. *World Economy.* 31:548-568.

Henson S and J Humphrey (2012). Private Standards in Global Agri-Food chains.9 In, Marx, A, Maertens M, Swinnen J and J Wouters (eds.). *Global Governance and Private Standards. Interdisciplinary Perspectives.* Cheltenham: Edward Elgar. 8-113.

Hiscox M J, Hainmueller J and Sequeira S (2015). Consumer Demand for the Fair Trade Label: Evidence from a Multi-Store Field Experiment. *Review of Economics and Statistics.* 97(2):242-256.

Hoang H T N, Hoshino S and Hashimoto S (2015) Forest stewardship council certificate for a group of planters in Vietnam: SWOT analysis and implications.Journal of Forest Research. 20(1): 35-42.

Hoekman B (2014). Supply Chains, Mega-Regionals and Multilateralism. A Road Map for the WTO. RSCAS Working Papers. European University Institute.

Holvoet B and B Muys (2004). Sustainable Forest Management Worldwide: A Comparative Assessment of Standards. *International Forestry Review*. 6(2):99–122.

Humphrey J (2008). Private Standards, Small Farmers and Donor Policies. EUREPGAP in Kenya. IDS Working Paper 308 IDS.

Irwin D (2020). Free Trade under Fire. 5th Edition. Princeton: Princeton University Press.

ISEAL (2010). Code of Good Practice for Setting Standards. London: ISEAL Alliance.

Jaffee S (2003). From Challenge to Opportunity: Transforming Kenyas Fresh Vegetable Trade in the Context of Emerging Food Safety and Other Standards in Europe. Agriculture and Rural Development discussion paper ; No. 2 Washington, D.C. : World Bank Group.

Kilian B, Jones C, Pratt L, Villalobos A (2006). Is sustainable agriculture a viable strategy to improve farm income in Central America? A case study on coffee. *Journal of Business Research*. 59 (3): 322–330. DOI: 10.1016/j.jbusres.2005.09.015.

Kilian B, Prat L, Jones C, Villalobos A (2004). Can the private sector be competitive and contribute to development through sustainable agricultural business? A case study of coffee in Latin America. *International Food and Agribusiness Management Review*. 7 (3):21–45.

Kim J Y (2013). The Politics of Code Enforcement and Implementation in Vietnams Apparel and Footwear Factories. *World Development*. 45:286-295.

Klooster D (2005). Environmental certification of forests: The evolution of environmental governance in a commodity network. *Journal of Rural Studies*. 21(4): 403-417.

Kowalski P, Gonzalez J L, Ragoussis A, and Ugarte C (2015). Participation of Developing Countries in Global Value Chains: Implications for Trade and Trade-Related Policies. OECD Trade Policy Papers, No. 179, OECD Publishing, ParisLambert S R, Elamin N, Fernandez de Cordoba S (2020).Maximizing sustainable agri-food supply chain opportunities to redress COVID-19 in developing countries. UNCTAD COVID-19 Response.

Lambin E and Thorlakson T (2018). Sustainability Standards: Interactions between private actors, civil society and governments. *Annual Review Environmental Resources*.43:369–393.

Lambin E Meyfroidt P, Rueda X, Blackman A, Börner J, Cerutti P, Dietsch T, Jungmann L, Lamarque P, Lister J, Walker N, and Wunder S (2014). Effectiveness and Synergies of Policy Instruments for Land Use Governance .*Tropical Regions Global Environmental Change*. 28:129-40.

Lambin E F, Meyfroidt P, Rueda X, Blackman A, Börner J, Cerutti P O (2014). Effectiveness and synergies of policy instruments for land use governance in tropical regions. *Global Environmental Change*. 28: 129–140. DOI: 10.1016/j.gloenvcha.2014.06.007.

Levi M, Adolph C, Berliner D, Erlich A, Greenleaf A, Lake M and Noveck J (2012). Aligning Rights and Interests: Why, When and How to Uphold Labor Standards. World Development Report 2013: Jobs Background Paper. Washington D.C., World Bank Levy D, Reinecke J and S Manning (2016). The Political Dynamics of Sustainable Coffee: Contested Value Regimes and the Transformation of Sustainability. *Journal of Management Studies*. 53(3):364-401.

Locke R and Romis M (2009). The Promise and Perils of Private Voluntary Regulation: Labor Standards and Work Organizations in Two Mexican Factories. *Review of International Political Economy*. 17(1):45-74.

Locke R (2013). The Promise and Limits of Private Power. Promoting Labor Standards in a Global Economy. Cambridge: Cambridge University Press.

Locke R, Amengual M and A. Mangla (2009). Virtue out of Necessity? Compliance, Commitment and the Improvement of Labor Conditions in Global Supply Chains. *Politics and Society*. 37(3):319-351.

Locke R M (2013). The Promise and Limits of Private Power. Cambridge: Cambridge University Press.

Locke R M, Romis M, (2010). The promise and perils of private voluntary regulation: Labor standards and work organization in two Mexican garment factories. *Review of International Political Economy*. 17 (1):45–74. DOI: 10.1080/09692290902893230.

Loconto and Dankers, (2014). Impact of International Voluntary Standards on Smallholder Market Participation in Developing Countries – A review of the literature. Rome: Food and Agriculture Organization of the United Nations.

Macdonald K (2020). Private sustainability standards as tools for empowering southern pro-regulatory coalitions? Collaboration, conflict and the pursuit of sustainable palm oil. *Ecological Economics*. 167.

Maertens M and J Swinnen (2012). Private standards, global food supply chains and the implications for developing countries..In Marx A, Maertens M, Swinnen J and Wouters J (eds.). *Global Governance and Private Standards. Interdisciplinary Perspectives*. Cheltenham: Edward Elgar. 153-171.

Mahaim (1934). The Historical and Social Importance of International Labour Legislation. In: Shotwell J (ed). *The Origins of the International Labour Organization*. Columbia University Press.

Mangelsdorf A (2011). The role of technical standards for trade between China and the European Union. *Technology Analysis and Strategic Management*. 23(7):725-743.

Maquila Solidarity Network (2005). Brand Campaigns and worker organizing. Toronto: Maquila Solidarity Network.

Marx A and D Cuypers (2010). Forest Certification as a Global Environmental Governance Tool. What is the Macro-impact of the Forest Stewardship Council. *Regulation and Governance*. 4(4):304-334.

Marques J C and Eberlein B (2020). Grounding transnational business governance: A political-strategic perspective on government responses in the Global South. *Regulation & Governance*.

Marx A (2008). Limits to non-state market regulation: A qualitative comparative analysis of the international sport footwear industry and the Fair Labor Association. *Regulation and Governance*. 2(2):253-273.

Marx A (2013). Varieties of Legitimacy: A Configurational Institutional Design Analysis of Eco-labels.*Innovation: European Journal for Social Science Research*. 26(3):268-287.

Marx A (2014). Legitimacy, Institutional Design and Dispute Settlement. The Case of Eco-certification systems. *Globalizations*. 11(3):401-416.

Marx A and Wouters J (2015). Competition and Cooperation in the Market of Voluntary Standards Sustainability Standards. In: Delimatsis P (ed.). *International standardization – Law, Economics and Politics*. Cambridge: Cambridge University Press, 215-241.

Marx A and Wouters J (2017). Intermediaries in Global Labour Governance. *The ANNALS of the American Academy of Political and Social Science*.670(1):189-206.

Marx A, Maertens M , Swinnen J, and Wouters J (eds.) (2012). Private Standards and Global Governance. Cheltenham Edward Elgar.

Masood A and Brümmer B (2014). Impact of GlobalGAP Certification on EU Banana Imports: GlobalFood Discussion Papers.

Mosley M (2011). Labor rights and multinational production. New York: Cambridge University Press.

Nadvi K, Lund-Thomsen P, Xue H and Khara N (2011). Playing against China: Global value chains and labour standards in the international sports goods industry. *Global Networks*. 3:334-354.

Naegele H (2020). Where does the Fair Trade money go? How much consumers pay extra for Fair Trade coffee and how this value is split along the value chain. *World Development*.133.

ORouke D (2012). Shopping for Good. MIT Press.

ORourke D (2000). Monitoring the Monitors: A Critique of PricewaterhouseCooper's Labor Monitoring. Available at https://respect.international/wp-content/uploads/2019/07/Monitoring-the-Monitors-A-Critique-of-PriceWaterhouseCoopers-PWC-Labor-Monitoring.pdf.

OECD (2020). Trade policy implications of global value chains. Available at https://www.oecd.org/trade/topics/global-value-chains-and-trade/#:~:text=In%20reality%2C%20about%2070%25%20of,consumers%20all%20over%20the%20world.

Oya C, Schaefer F, Skalidou D (2018). The effectiveness of agricultural certification in developing countries: A systematic review. *World Development*. 112:282–312. DOI: 10.1016/j.worlddev.2018.08.001.

Parkes G, Young J A, Walmsley S F, Abel R, Harman J , Horvat P (2010). Behind the Signs—A Global Review of Fish Sustainability Information Schemes. *Reviews in Fisheries Science*. 18 (4):344–356. DOI: 10.1080/10641262.2010.516374.

Partiti E (2021). The effects of human rights due diligence on voluntary sustainability standards, paper presented at the conference The evolution of transnational private rule-makers: Understanding drivers and dynamics Tilburg.

Pinto L F G and McDermott C (2013). Equity and Forest Certification – A case study in Brazil in. *Forest Policy and Economics*. 30: 23-29.

Ponte S (2008). Greener Than Thou: The political economy of fish ecolabeling and its local manifestations in South Africa. *World Development*. 36(1):159–175.

Ponte S (2019). Business, Power and Sustainability in a World of Global Value Chains: A History of Power, Politics and Profit. Chicago: Zed Books Ltd.

Potoski M and Prakash A (2005). Green clubs and voluntary governance: ISO 14001 and firms regulatory compliance. *American Journal of Political Science*. 49(2):235–248.

Putzel L, Dermawan A, Moeliono M and Trung L Q (2012). Improving opportunities for smallholder timber planters in Vietnam to benefit from domestic wood processing. *International Forestry Review*.14(2):227-237.

Raynolds L T, Murray D, Leigh T (2004). Fair trade coffee: building producer capacity via global networks. *Journal of International Development*. 16(8): 1109–1121. DOI: 10.1002/jid.1136.

Reinecke J, Manning S, O von Hagen (2012). The Emergence of a Standards Market: Multiplicity of Sustainability Standards in the Global Coffee Industry. *Organization Studies*. 335-6): 791–814. DOI: 10.1177/0170840612443629.

Renckens S and G Auld (2019). Structure, Path Dependence, and Adaptation: North-South Imbalances in Transnational Private Fisheries Governance. *Ecological Economics*.166.

Renckens S (2020). Private Governance and Public Authority: Regulating Sustainability in a Global Economy. Cambridge: Cambridge University Press. doi:10.1017/9781108781015.

Robertson R, Brown D and Dehejia R (2011). Working Conditions and Factory Survival: Evidence from Better Factories Cambodia. *Review of development Economics*. 25.

Rosen E (2002). Making Sweatshops. The Globalization of the U.S. Apparel Industry. Berkeley: University of California Press.

Ruerd R (2008)(ed.). The Impact of Fair Trade. Wageningen Academic Publishers.

Ruerd R, Fort R, and Zúniga-Arias G (2009). Measuring the Impact of Fair Trade on Development. *Development in Practice*. 19(6) 777-788.

Sabatier Paul A (1986). Top-Down and Bottom-Up Approaches to Implementation Research: a Critical Analysis and Suggested Synthesis. *Journal of Public Policy*. 6(1):21–48. Online verfügbar unter https://EconPapers.repec.org/RePEc:cup:jnlpup:v:6:y:1986:i:01:p:21-48_00.

Sabel C, O'Rourke D and Fung A (2000). Ratcheting Labor Standards. Regulation for Continuous Improvement in the Global Workplace. Columbia Law School. The Center for Law and Economic Studies Working Paper No. 185.

Schleifer P, Fiorini M and Fransen L (2019). Missing the Bigger Picture: A Population-level Analysis of Transnational Private Governance Organizations Active in the Global South. *Ecological Economics*. 164.

Schneider A and Ingram H (1990). Behavioral Assumptions of Policy Tools. *The Journal of Politics*. 52(2): 510–529. DOI: 10.2307/2131904.

Schouten G and Bitzer V (2015). The Emergence of Southern standards in agricultural value chains: a new trend in sustainability governance. *Ecological Economics*. 120:175-184.

Sellare J, Meemken E M, Kouamé C and Qaim M (2020). Do Sustainability Standards Benefit Smallholder Farmers Also When Accounting For Cooperative Effects? Evidence from Côte dIvoire. *American Journal of Agricultural Economics*.102 (2): 681–695. DOI: 10.1002/ajae.12015.

Servais J M (2011). The International Labour Organization, Wouters J (ed.), *International Encyclopedia of Laws: Intergovernmental Organizations*. Deventer: Kluwer, 3rd ed., 2011.

Stanton G (2012). Food safety-related private standards: the WTO perspective. , In Marx A et al. (eds.) *Global Governance and Private Standards. Interdisciplinary Perspectives*. Cheltenham: Edward Elgar. 235-254.

Starobin S (2021). Credibility beyond compliance: uncertified smallholders in sustainable food systems. *Ecological Economics*. 180.

Stratoudakis Y, McConney P, Duncan J, Ghofar A, Gitonga N, Mohamed K S and and Bourillon L (2016). Fisheries certification in the developing world: Locks and keys or square pegs in round holes? *Fisheries Research*. 182:39–49.

Swan G P (2010). International Standards and Trade: A Review of the Empirical Literature. OECD Trade Policy Working Papers. https://doi.org/10.1787/5kmdbg9xktwg-en.

Swinnen J F M (2007). Global supply chains, standards and the poor: How the globalization of food systems and standards affects rural development and poverty. KU Leuven, Belgium.

Tayleur C M, Balmford A, Buchanan G, Butchart S H M, Corlet Walker C, Ducharme H ,Green R Milder J, Sanderson F, Thomas D H L Tracewski L, Vickery J and Phalan B (2018). Where are commodity crops certified, and what does it mean for conservation and poverty alleviation? *Biological Conservation*. 217:36-46. 10.17863/CAM.22719.

Tayleur C M, Balmford A, Buchanan G, Butchart SHM, Ducharme H, Green R and Milder J, Sanderson F,Thomas, Vickery J and Phalan B (2016). Global Coverage of Agricultural Sustainability Standards, and Their Role in Conserving Biodiversity. *Conservation Letters*. 10(5):619-618. 10. 10.1111/conl.12314.

Tröster R and Hiete M (2018): Success of voluntary sustainability certification schemes – A comprehensive review. *Journal of Cleaner Production*. 196:1034–1043. DOI: 10.1016/j.jclepro.2018.05.240.

United Nations General Assembly, Transforming our world: the 2030 Agenda for Sustainable Development, 21 October 2015, A/RES/70/1. Available at https://www.un.org/ga/search/view_doc.asp?symbol=A/RES/70/1andLang=E.

UNCTAD (2016). *Trading into Sustainable Development: Trade, Market Access, and the Sustainable Development Goals, Developing Countries in International Trade Studies* (United Nations Publication ISSN 1817-1214. New York and Geneva).

UNCTAD (2018). *The Least Developed Countries Report 2018: Entrepreneurship for Structural Transformation – Beyond Business as Usual* (United Nations publication. Sales No. E.18.II.D.6. New York and Geneva) .

UNCTAD (2019a). *Key statistics and trends in international trade* (United Nations publication. Sales No.: E.21.II.D.6 Geneva).

UNCTAD (2019b). *Trade Policies for Compating Inequality* (United Nations Publication Sales No. E.19.II.D.21 Geneva).

UNCTAD, OECD, and WTO (2013). *Implications of global value chains for trade, investment, development and jobs*. Available at https://unctad.org/system/files/official-document/unctad_oecd_wto_2013d1_en.pdf.

UNFSS (2013). Voluntary Sustainability Standards. Today's Landscape of Issues and Initiatives to Achieve Public Policy Objectives. Geneva: United Nations Forum on Sustainability Standards. Available at https://unfss.org/home/flagship-publication/.

UNFSS (2016). Meeting Sustainability Goals. Voluntary sustainability standards and the role of the government.. Geneva: United Nations Forum on Sustainability Standards. Available At https://unfss.files.wordpress.com/2016/09/final_unfss-report_28092016.pdf.

UNFSS (2018). Voluntary Sustainability Standards, Trade and Sustainable Development. Geneva: United Nations Forum on Sustainability Standards.

UNFSS (2020). Scaling up VSS through Sustainable Public Procurement and Trade Policy. Geneva: United Nations Forum on Sustainability Standards.

Unnevehr L J (2000). Food safety issues and fresh food product exports from LDCs. *Agricultural Economics*. 23(3):231-240.

Van der Ven H (2019). Beyond Greenwash. Explaining Credibility in Transnational Eco-Labeling. Oxford: Oxford University Press.

Vogel A (2005). The Market for Virtue: The Potential and Limits of Corporate Social Responsibility, Washington DC: Brookings Institutions.

Vogel D(2008). Private Global Business Regulation. Annual Review of Political Science. 11(1):261–282. DOI: 10.1146/annurev.polisci.11.053106.141706.

Von Essen M and Lambin E (2021). Jurisdictional Approached to Sustainable Resource Use. *Frontiers in Ecology and the Environment*. 19(3): 159-167.

Willer H, Sampson G, Voora V, Dang D, Lernoud J (2019). The State of Sustainable Markets 2019 – Statistics and Emerging Trends. ITC, Geneva.

World Bank (2008). *World Development Report. Agriculture for Development*. World Bank . Washington, D.C.

World Bank (2020). *World Development Report 2020. Trading for Development in the Age of Global Value Chains*. World Bank . Washington, D.C.

World Commission on the Social Dimension of Globalization (2004). A Fair Globalization: Creating Opportunity for All. ILO. Geneva, available at www.ilo.org/public/English/wcsdg/docs/report.pdf.

WTO (2018). *Mainstreaming trade to attain the Sustainable Development Goals*. WTO. Geneva. Available at https://www.wto.org/english/res_e/booksp_e/sdg_e.pdf.

WTO (2019). *Global Value Chain Development Report: Technological innovation, Supply Chain Trade, and Workers in a Globalized World*. Available at https://www.wto.org/english/res_e/booksp_e/gvc_dev_report_2019_e.pdf.

WTO (2020). *THE COVID-19 PANDEMIC AND TRADE-RELATED DEVELOPMENTS IN LDCs*. Information note. Available at https://www.wto.org/english/tratop_e/covid19_e/ldcs_report_e.pdf.

WTO (2021). *COVID-19 AND GLOBAL VALUE CHAINS A DISCUSSION OF ARGUMENTS ON VALUE CHAIN ORGANIZATION AND THE ROLE OF THE WTO*. Retrieved from https://www.wto.org/english/res_e/reser_e/ersd202103_e.pdf.

WWF (2017). SDGs Mean Business: *How Credible Standards Can Help Companies Deliver the 2030 Agenda*. WWF-ISEAL joint report. Gland, Switzerland. Available at https://wwfint.awsassets.panda.org/downloads/wwf_iseal_sdg_2017_28_feb.pdf.

ANNEX

It has been made clear by existing reviews that the scholarly literature that has empirically assessed the effectiveness of VSS on certified production sites is highly limited to VSS in three subsectors: forestry, (tropical) farm agriculture, and fisheries/aquaculture (Tröster und Hiete 2018). Following these insights, the TRANS SUSTAIN project at the University of Münster (Germany) has identified and evaluated a comprehensive literature base that includes scholarly articles focusing on the sustainability effects of VSS on certified production within these three sub-sectors.

This literature base was developed in three steps. First, the TRANS SUSTAIN project compiled a list of major VSS within the three mentioned sectors that are widely assumed to have developed into vital governance mechanisms (see table below). Second, the different VSS were combined in a search string that was used to trawl Scopus, a widely-used scientific database. With this strategy, TRANS SUSTAIN identified all articles available through Scopus that analyzed one or more of the major certification schemes previously selected, yielding 2,913 results.

Table A1. Overview of major VSS in the forestry, farm-agriculture and fisheries/aquaculture sector included into the TRANS SUSTAIN literature base

Sub-sector	Sustainability certifications
Forestry	• Forest Stewardship Council (FSC) • Program for the Endorsement of Forest Certification (PEFC) • Sustainable Forestry Initiative (SFI)
Farm-agriculture	• Roundtable on Sustainable Palm Oil (RSPO) • GlobalGAP • Rainforest Alliance (RFA) • UTZ • Roundtable on Responsible Soy (RTRS) • Fairtrade (FT) • Fairtrade/Organic (FTorg) • 4C • Better Cotton Initiative (BCI) • Cotton made in Africa (CMA) • Bonsucro
Fisheries/aquaculture	• Global Aquaculture Alliance (GAA) • Friends of the Sea (FoS) • Marine Stewardship Council (MSC) • Aquaculture Stewardship Council

Third, TRANS SUSTAIN screened this literature with an inclusive screening approach. Each article that presented and evaluated some kind of empirical evidence to assess the state of social, economic or environmental sustainability in a certified production sites was selected. Explicitly, the screening strategy allowed for the selection of both (quasi-)experimental impact evaluation studies alongside non-experimental approaches. Overall, this screening process led to a literature base of in total 176 articles. The TRANSUSTAIN project has structured the articles according to a number of coding categories (see table below)

Table A2. Coding scheme set by the TRANS SUSTAIN project to analyze VSS effectiveness and impacts

Coding area	Coding categories
Research Design	
Research approach	Quantitative (quasi)-experimental, qualitative (quasi)-experimental, Quantitative non-experimental, Qualitative non-experimental, meta-study
Data sources	Direct observations, surveys (large n), in-depth interviews, documents
Time Dimension	
Year of publication	Years 2000-2020
Scope Dimension	
Individual SCs	See SCs in Table 1.
Type of SCs	NGO/Civil Society-driven SCs, Corporate/Business Association-driven SCs
Sustainability area of investigated outcome variable	Environmental, social or economic outcome variables
Agricultural sub-sector	Forest, farm-agriculture, fisheries/aquaculture
Business sector of certified production site	Timber, coffee, seafood, palm oil, tea, cocoa, multiple/other
Development status of certified production site	Smallholder, non-smallholder
Country of Certified production site / differentiated according to institutional strength	all countries possible
Depth Dimension	
Intermediate vs. end-point outcomes	Intermediate outcome variable, end-point outcome variables
Implementation costs investigated outcome variable	High, middle or low implementation costs

TRANS SUSTAIN coded code 1 if one of the categories specified above occurs an article. Each time a category occurs in an article presents a case that TRANS SUSTAIN counted and analyzed separately. Counting the number of cases per category makes it possible to understand how the evidence base is structured, and to identify crucial knowledge gaps. The more cases one find for a category the better is the evidence base for this coding category, while coding categories that have only rarely or not been addressed by the pertinent literature present significant knowledge gaps.

Next, TRANS SUSTAIN code for all occurrences of a category (cases) whether they are linked to a positive (coding 1), mixed (coding 2) or negative evaluation (coding 1) and calculate the distribution of positive, mixed and negative assessments per coding category. In doing so, TRANS SUSTAIN analyzes the extent to which a particular category co-relates with a particular evaluation. As a result, step by step a highly nuanced picture emerges about how the pertinent literature assesses the effectiveness of VSS. For a complete overview of results generated through this meta-study on VSS effectiveness and impacts analysis please contact: thomas.dietz@uni-muenster.de. In this report, we summarize some of the main findings of this meta-study.